MW01152209

The Legacy
of
Master Nuno Oliveira

by Stephanie Grant Millham

With an Introduction

by SYLVIA LOCH

XENOPHON PRESS

Title: *The Legacy of Master Nuno Oliveira*
by Stephanie Grant Millham

Copyright © 2013 by Xenophon Press LLC

Edited by Richard F. Williams

Published by Xenophon Press LLC

7518 Bayside Road, Franktown, Virginia 23354-2106, U.S.A.

XenophonPress@gmail.com

ISBN-10   0933316348
ISBN-13   978-0-933316-34-8

Cover design by Naia Poyer.

TABLE OF CONTENTS

Xenophon Press Library

30 Years with Master Nuno Oliveira, Michel Henriquet, 2011
Another Horsemanship, Jean-Claude Racinet, 1994
A Rider's Survival from Tyranny, Charles de Kunffy, 2012
Art of the Lusitano, Pedro Yglesias de Oliveira, 2012
Baucher and His School, General Decarpentry, 2011
Dressage in the French Tradition, Dom Diogo de Bragança, 2011
École de Cavalerie Part II (School of Horsemanship),
        François Robichon de la Guérinière, 1992
François Baucher, The Man and His Method, Hilda Nelson, 2013
*From the Real Picaria of the 18th Century to the Portuguese School of
        Equestrian Art*, Yglesias de Oliverira and da Costa, 2012
Gymnastic Exercises for Horses Volume II, Eleanor Russell, 2013
Healing Hands, Dominique Giniaux, DVM, 1998
*Methodical Dressage of the Riding Horse, and Dressage of the Outdoor
        Horse*, Faverot de Kerbrech, 2010
Racinet Explains Baucher, Jean-Claude Racinet, 1997
The Écuyère of the Nineteenth Century in the Circus, Hilda Nelson
        2001
The Ethics and Passions of Dressage, Expanded Edition,
        Charles de Kunffy, 2013
The Gymnasium of the Horse, Gustav Steinbrecht, 2011
The Handbook of Jumping Essentials,
        François Lemaire de Ruffieu, 1997
The Legacy of Master Nuno Oliveira, Stephanie Grant Millham, 2013
The Maneige Royal, Antoine de Pluvinel, 2010
The Spanish Riding School in Vienna and Piaffe and Passage,
        General Decarpentry, 2013
The Wisdom of Master Nuno Oliveira, Antoine de Coux, 2012
Total Horsemanship, Jean-Claude Racinet, 1999
What the Horses Have Told Me, Dominique Giniaux, DVM, 1996

Available at **www.XenophonPress.com**

INTRODUCTION

By Sylvia Loch

It is always a great honor to be invited to write an Introduction to a book in which one believes. I have been fortunate to be placed in this position four times in my life and two of those were new editions of the work of the late great Colonel Alois Podhajsky—with whom I had a special connection through friends at the Spanish Riding School and particularly his wife, Eva. Sadly that particular Master had passed away long before my first pilgrimage to Vienna. Nevertheless, I felt his presence was still very much there and he talks straight to you through his books.

Far away in Portugal, another Master was practicing his art. Work as ancient as the hills, laid down by successive generations of master horsemen—followed by schools as old as Vienna and later Versailles and Lisbon—was being kept alive. Did the ghost of Podhajsky touch the proceedings here? Was it possible the Colonel's friendship with 'our Nuno' had woven a peculiar magic? Who knows? All we knew was the constancy of the same principles, the commitment to work within nature's laws, where each movement, every exercise is governed by gravity, was exactly the same. Whether it was Oliveira or Podhajsky, the practice of fine equitation, built up over centuries to protect the horse yet at the same time train him to a state of brilliance, is an inspiration to us all.

People flocked to see it. At Nuno Oliveira's, there was no grand architecture, no lofty portals and arches through which a king might ride. Instead, a small indoor school, set on a steep rugged pathway up a Portuguese hillside, was simplicity itself. Yet, the gallery at Quinta do Brejo was always full, the courses overflowing and people came from all over the world. As Stephanie indicates in her book...'When the student is ready the master teacher appears.'

Reading Stephanie's book brings back all the memories. I was lucky enough to live at a time when the Master, Nuno Oliveira, was very much alive. A vibrant man, a living, breathing *Mestre*—the Portuguese word—a man of immense energy and charm—you could not forget him. Long before he placed his foot in the stirrup, you knew he was special—but that is an understatement. On a horse, Nuno Oliveira was simply quite unique.

There had been the fleeting visits, the glimpses from the intimate gallery, the knowing conversations teacher to teacher with my late husband Lord Henry Loch, a former cavalry instructor. My own chance to get to know the *Mestre* better, talk one to one, came later. I received a letter from his daughter Pureza indicating that her father could be interested in my coming to the Quinta with the purpose of writing a book—a biography no less.

I was dispatched to Lisbon by my publishers with considerable enthusiasm. I was to stay at Mafra, in a pleasant enough hotel but dinner at night was at the Oliveira family home and I remember watching a number of grainy videos over a glass of red wine in front of a fire while Oliveira's grandchildren—now serious horsemen in the family tradition—moved quietly in the background. You wouldn't dare do otherwise in such a patriarchal atmosphere.

Many words were spoken but often out of context. He had a habit of changing the subject when a direct question was asked. In the mode of his first book *Reflections*, the sentences were short, sometimes random. But for meaning, read the expressive hands, the eyebrows, the shrug of the shoulder and nod of the head; they said a lot. 'We will talk again,' he always said and I worried as he did not seem quite the same person I remembered from the last time I had set foot in Avessada. Neither of us could guess that a year later he would not be there, cut down in his prime—you could say—far away in Australia. Sadly, we had not finished those conversations. In many ways, they had hardly begun.

Stephanie's book is a masterpiece. Her time spent with the *Mestre* considerable which allowed her to glean from a programme that would take her and her horse Raindrop to heights they would never otherwise have dreamed of. How refreshing! And how different from the countless riders who spent just a week here or a week there and then claimed they were 'students of Oliveira' only to capitalize on it ever since—often teaching the very opposite of what the *Mestre* intended. To my mind, real students of Oliveira were few and far between and mainly Portuguese, with the odd exception such as Michel Henriquet of France, Danny Pevsner now in England, Bettina Drummond, USA, Joy Howley, Australia and the author of this book.

What I like in these pages is the lucid, conversational style and the sights and sounds that were so much part of Quinta do Brejo. The grey stallion on relaxed reins, Nuno sitting in his corner with the 'ubiquitous cigarette,' and of course the opera often cascading in the background. But even more important than these are the insights. Stephanie has put these into a logical and meaningful form so that the quotes spring out at you and you want to cry 'YES!'

One of the hardest things to convey to one's own students is that contact may be constant but it must never be fixed. The contradictions are obvious but all life is a contradiction and horsemanship no different. The word 'core' in relation to the rider's body was not prevalent in those days, but Oliveira's meaning was clear when he wrote 'Push your back and stomach forward and keep the rein for a moment, a fraction of a second. Take and give with the fingers. If you don't relax after a second, the horse resists.'

And because the horse should always continue in the same frame, the same mode as you do this, today's riders often don't get it. They don't understand the need for the 'take and give' and think that constancy of contact is to do with maintaining so many pounds of weight in their hand which never changes and which, of course, does nothing for the horse's mouth. As Stephanie points out, the *Mestre* was adamant that 'there should be no confusion between this heavy tension on the bit and the necessary light contact which activates the rein'—and indeed activates the horse.

Of course, watching Oliveira on a horse left one in no doubt that he used his back and his stomach (or core) to great effect. I remember long ago, on a first visit to his stable back in the 1970s what a big man he looked on the stallion he was riding at the time. He dominated it with his presence, but never his aids. When he dismounted, I was expecting a very tall man, 6 ft. 1" or 6 ft. 2" for instance. What came as such a surprise was the fact he was no bigger than my husband Henry who was 5 ft. 10", just an inch taller than me. It was Oliveira's posture which made him big, puffed up and proud. No wonder Stephanie compares him to that famous portrait of Nestier, *écuyer* to Louis XV of France. Forget the powdered wig, the frock coat and the tricorn hat—it was the poise that did it for me and visualizing that truly centered position in my own riding has helped me time and again to sit still, quiet and let go with the aids. The *descente de jambes* and *descente de mains* are certainly as meaningful now—perhaps more so for dressage horses—than they ever were in the times of the great high priests of classical riding and indeed at Quinta do Brejo.

Stephanie's book reaches deep into the heart of the Portuguese countryside. Having lived there for 10 years myself, I deeply appreciate her skill at summing up pictures, too often forgotten. One of my favorite paragraphs in the book is where, in times of trouble with a difficult student, a difficult horse...., she takes herself back to the past. 'In my mind's eye I walk again the dusty track from the rural village of Avessada, strolling past donkey carts, past cows being driven to water, up and down the picturesque Portuguese hills on the way to the Master's arena. On my way I may encounter a groom leading a beautiful Lusitano to the farm, or a donkey set loose to graze. Once I have set the scene in such a meditative moment, an appropriate quote usually comes to mind. I remember the Master's deep relaxing tone of voice, his immovable calm, and I know that with knowledge, time and patience a solution always comes.'

And that, in a way, sums up the whole of this beautiful and important book. Not only is there so much to share and learn, it is one of which the *Mestre* himself would be immensely proud.

Sylvia Loch

Accredited Instructor of the Portuguese National Federation,

Honorary President and Founder of The Lusitano Breed Society

of Great Britain, and of The Classical Riding Club

AUTHOR'S PREFACE

There is an old adage that proclaims when the student is ready, the master teacher will appear. Some thirty-five years ago, as an assistant editor for the weekly magazine *The Chronicle of the Horse*, I was extremely fortunate to be in the right place at the right time to meet the man already being called "the Master" who would become the greatest influence in my riding career. An avid scholar of equestrian literature as well as an active rider, I was in search of a worthy mentor to guide my own personal journey into the higher realms of dressage.

When a review copy of Nuno Oliveira's *Reflections on Equestrian Art* (J. A. Allen, 1976) came across my editorial desk, I knew I need look no further. I devoured the book in one sitting, and realized instantly I needed to meet this man who had penned the greatest work on classical equitation I had yet encountered. In one of those blessed events of synchronicity, it transpired that the gentleman from Portugal was scheduled to conduct a clinic in my area not too far in the future, and thus arrangements were made to audit the clinic and also to conduct an interview with the renowned trainer.

That first interview led to a series of ongoing articles in various equestrian magazines on Mr. Oliveira's philosophies and techniques of dressage. From that time I became a regular student at his American clinics and was also invited to study with him in Portugal, and so for ten years I was extremely privileged to learn under the man the world called simply "the Master."

Today, nearly a quarter century after his death, at a time when the dressage world is hungry for the ideals of kindness and lightness he espoused, it is especially gratifying to see a renewed interest in his teachings and his works. While the English editions of most of his books are currently out of print, we are fortunate that Xenophon Press is now publishing the English translations of books by a number of his foreign students. This work represents an original American addition to the series, compiled from many interviews and conversations with the Master along with years of notes from his lessons.

In compiling such a work, it is important to give credit to those whose inspiration and input have contributed so much to passing on the legacy of Nuno Oliveira. I would like to give special acknowledgment, in no particular order, to a few of those individuals without whose kindness and belief this project would not have come to fruition.

Thanks to my dear friend and colleague Holly Hansen, who kept insisting over the years that this book be written, and to Nadja King, editor of *Horses for Life* magazine, who reprinted some of the original material and kept demanding more.

Special kudos to my husband Ernie, who spent endless hours on the computer, and to Melinda Neese, who helped reclaim many of the old photos.

Thanks especially to Pureza Oliveira, Nuno Oliveira's daughter, for graciously allowing the use of many of the old photographs that appear in this book. Thanks also to Kathy Nelson and to Sally and Kathy Cleaver, who took most of the later photos. Special thanks to many of Mr. Oliveira's students and friends who shared stories and notes about their experiences with the Master over the years.

The American dressage community owes a huge debt of gratitude to Phyllis Field and the Sant' Agata Foundation who sponsored the clinics in America with Mr. Oliveira and also provided scholarships for so many talented young trainers to study with him in Portugal. In keeping with her wishes, we are passing it on.

Finally, thanks to my own students and horses, who proved time and again the truth of his teachings, and most importantly, heartfelt thanks to Nuno Oliveira himself for his genius, his generosity, his friendship, his artistry, and his incomparable wisdom.

He is sorely missed.

Stephanie Millham

Rixeyville, VA

December 2012

Chapter 1

CONVERSATIONS WITH A MASTER

The grey stallion walks calmly on loose reins, occasionally mouthing his bits with a gentle clink. Quietly the rider picks up the reins without changing position, though his mount grows suddenly animated, collecting himself for a canter depart. A moment later—again with only the most discreet aids, barely visible to those in the gallery—horse and rider skip down the long side of the arena in a series of fluid flying changes every stride.

Another walk on loose reins follows; then the rider establishes collection and the stallion lifts into a majestic, effortless passage—high, cadenced, with almost incredible suspension—that seems as if he could hold it forever. The figures that follow, circles and half-pass, are executed in the same never-faltering rhythm of the passage.

"Enough," murmurs Nuno Oliveira as he drops the reins again and offers the expected sugar upon dismounting. It is a reunion of sorts between the grey Lusitano, exported to America, and the Portuguese dressage master who trained him in the airs of the *haute école*. The year is 1982, only seven years before his death, and he has returned once again, as he has done for many years, to work with a small group of dedicated students fortunate enough to study with him, often for two weeks at a time, four or more times a year, during his clinics in the United States.

He is gone now—almost impossible to believe that as I write this we are nearing the 25th anniversary of his death—but the legacy of the man often called the greatest classical master of the twentieth century lives on, not only in his books but in the memory and teachings of his students. He was genuinely a man greatly ahead of his time, and his true worth is only beginning to be recognized in this age that longs for a return to lightness and grace and—dare we say it— love in our modern contentious horse world.

Refreshingly honest, Nuno Oliveira was a master teacher who shared his philosophy and unique insights as well as his technical expertise with those students who cared to listen in his many lessons all over the world and in conversations that appeared in a series of articles thirty years ago that are as timely now as they were then. Although the technical information in itself is priceless, it is the pearls of wisdom found in his philosophy that will most probably define his unique place in equestrian history.

Portrait of a Master

A Master's Words

"The Americans have changed me," laughs Nuno Oliveira ruefully. It is a damp, chilly morning in 1979 in Portugal in early spring, and we are sitting in the gallery of his small indoor school, huddled around the electric heater as he looks through a folder of photos I have taken for a series of articles, choosing a few he likes that will appear in the upcoming French edition of one of his books.

The gallery is a delightful and charming place. Italian opera, his favorite, plays softly in the background. Casement windows look down into the 15 x 30 meter indoor school, which is currently empty, as we wait for the morning's first group lesson to hack up the hill from the stables below.

Riding with "the Master," as he is often called, is not for the faint-hearted. Students accustomed only to the confines of a fenced arena may experience a bit of culture shock upon immediately being mounted on one of his schoolmasters, falling into line, and following a group of other stallions up the steep hill to his *manège*, located about an hour's drive from Lisbon. If it is the first lesson on Monday morning after a day off, some of the younger stallions may be quite exuberant on their trek up the hill. It is definitely an advantage to have some experience riding cross-country.

3

We laugh and joke with each other and Mr. Oliveira as we wait for the riders to arrive. Because of the early hour and the time of year, the gallery is not full, so there is an intimate air with conversations flowing quietly in several languages, mostly English and French this day. Where silence used to reign, thanks to the more outspoken Americans there is a friendlier, more relaxed air of informality. "It used to be too much like a cathedral in here," someone volunteers, and Nuno smiles and laughs softly. Yes, the Americans, and also the Australians, have changed the face of one of the world's great private classical schools, and I feel both privileged and humbled on this particular morning to be part of that change.

The conversation resumes. Unlike some other interviews we have done, sitting there with a tape player recording every word, the atmosphere today is casual. These mornings with the Master, and the traditional evenings over a glass of wine in his office after the last ride of the day, are precious. Without the tape rolling, as scribe I attempt to capture every word. Already, I have the feeling, perhaps a sense of *déjà vu*, that one day these sessions will be invaluable and I will strive to remember every moment.

"Dressage," he is explaining emphatically as the morning ride bounces into the arena, "is not to have only the movements, to show half-pass, shoulder-in, flying changes, passage and piaffer. Dressage is to have the horse relaxed, with a good feeling, and if dressage is good, the horse becomes better balanced for other things, such as jumping. That's dressage. The body is relaxed because the mind is relaxed. Both things are important."

Relaxation of the rider, which helps achieve both relaxation and remarkable impulsion in the horse, was always a key ingredient in his instruction to students, both on his school horses in Portugal and on their own horses in his clinics all over the world. A page from my journal, penned some thirty-three years ago on that chilly morning, reads: Lesson one is *Relaxation*.

Early spring in Portugal, my diary continues, is the rainy season and one of the best times to go for instruction, since it is not so busy as the rest of the year. The group during this stay is neither large nor small. As students ride twice a day, there are two group lessons in the morning and two in the afternoon. Our group this particular trip is made up of a delightfully motley assembly: five Frenchmen, two British instructors, two Canadians, a Spanish horse breeder, and nine Americans, including a number of dressage and three-day-event instructors.

Our real "home" for the duration of our stay is Nuno Oliveira's lovely farm, Quinta do Brejo (literally, "farm of the marsh") tucked among the steep, verdant hills and overlooking an orange grove. More specifically, we "live" in the arena, a pleasant half-mile walk from the village of Avessada, where some of us have rooms. As Mr. Oliveira begins work at 7 a.m. and continues till 7 or 8 p.m., there is ample time to absorb as much as one wishes.

The stables, my journal continues, are white slab, like almost everything in Portugal, with red tile roofs. The arena is one-quarter open at the top, with pillars leading to a high ceiling. There is excellent lighting, convenient mirrors, and bright green wooden doors. The gallery is up a steep flight of stairs and a gem with its two-tiered wooden benches, classical silhouettes and old bits along the walls. The hospitality corner and electric heaters keep everything cozy.

A mirror hangs over the entrance doors, and on either side are blue tile plaques – *azulejos* – of Nuno, one in levade, one piaffer to complete the ambiance. His office, where we go each evening for those long discussions over Portuguese wine, is a real haven at the end of each day's work, my diary concludes, and I remember it so very well to this day. How I treasure and miss those enlightening discussions that exposed so many to an equestrian culture, hard to find in this modern age.

Nuno Oliveira trained horses in classical dressage, including all the Grand Prix movements and the Airs above the Ground, for almost 60 years. It is said that he probably trained more horses to the highest levels than any other master of the art. The horses he produced exhibited the acme of true collection and were incredibly light in hand. What is not generally known is that his background also included experience with jumpers, and that he believed that jumping is vital to a *rider's* development.

The horses file into the arena. One dark grey stallion toward the end of the line jumps around a bit in an expression of *joie de vivre*. The rider calms him and quietly resumes her place in line. "Before a rider can be good in dressage," Mr. Oliveira reiterates on that chilly morning, "he should jump. Jump a lot, and go forward, and afterwards start dressage. It's ridiculous that in modern days there are so many riders all over the world who want to start dressage but are afraid to jump. Go forward first!"

Quinta do Brejo, Nuno Oliveira's school near the village of Avessada

Why Do We Ride?

Mr. Oliveira tells the story of once stopping a class of riders and asking them, "Why do you ride?" Dissatisfied with the technical answers he received, he replied: "You ride because you love your horse. Outside rein, inside rein is nothing. It is important to have feeling, and to love horses."

"Schooling is to relax the mind and body of the horse. You don't ride your competition movements every day. If you work all things every day, you mechanize the horse, and he begins to worry, 'I must do all these things....' Keep the mind fresh, and if he gets upset after an exercise, do something easy to relax."

As a teacher, Mr. Oliveira wasted few words. Consequently, his students learned that what he did say was doubly important, not only to correct their own general riding faults but to correct specific problems and to aid their further progress in schooling their own horses at home as well.

"The idea of each schooling session should not be to show many different movements to the instructor or the gallery, but to prepare the horse for the specific work planned for the day," he instructs.

"You must work the body of the horse, but you must also consider the mind. You should ask yourself every day, 'What does my horse think of me?' When he resists, you discipline at that moment, but it is never brutal. Horses know whether or not the rider is kind. It is important to be kind."

A tireless worker, and also an erudite scholar with an encyclopedic knowledge of the equestrian classics, Mr. Oliveira was a true genius at selecting the right exercise at the right moment for each horse and rider. If you were a serious rider, which he appreciated, and not just a dilettante who wanted to ride a few advanced movements, he was also famous for choosing the right schoolmasters from his stable to address your weaknesses as a rider, whether mental or physical, to further your development. He exhorted serious students to read and study the classic works not only of French horsemen such as L'Hotte, Baucher and Beudant, but also the German master, Gustav Steinbrecht.

A groom leads a horse from the village past the Master's house for an early morning schooling session.

**Three Portuguese stallions await their schooling session
under the Master.**

Incredibly open-minded, he had an exercise for everything, and one could never describe him as fitting into a box with only one technique. Perhaps his work is best described by the late French writer Jean-Claude Racinet who, although not a student of the Master, wisely put it: "Thus the Portuguese style Oliveira was the illustration of could be considered as a synthesis of the two great French equerries, La Guérinière in the 18th century and Baucher in the 19th century." In his article on Nuno Oliveira[9] in the April 1995 issue of *Dressage & CT* magazine, *"Was Oliveira a Baucherist?"* Racinet concludes "he was the most complete, the most knowledgeable riding Master that ever was." Other writers have referred to this mastery as "a moderate Baucherism grafted onto a classical trunk" and see him as a bridge between the old classical masters and the modern horseman.

This vast repertoire of knowledge allowed him to train each horse according to its unique needs and individual progression.

"You train a horse with simple, not complicated things," he repeated often. "Riders sometimes forget little things, but these little

9   See Chapter 8 for further excerpts on Nuno Oliveira and Baucher.

points are very important when you work a horse. A circle must be round, not like an egg or a potato!"

"Ride with discipline, not force. Solve all problems with appropriate exercises, not force."

"Every exercise develops certain muscles. Shoulder-in and counter shoulder-in develop some. Half-pass develops some. First comes the crossing of the legs, then the bend, and afterwards the horse can be round."

Although the lightness he achieved in all breeds was legendary, of equal importance should be noted the incredible suppleness he gave his horses.

His delicate, tactful use of lateral flexion and the full release of the horse's top line were second to none, and have certainly remained my ideal over the years. I remember his words like a mantra when he was dealing with a stiff horse and rider in a clinic situation: "You must bend the horse."

Different exercises and different horses require different bend, of course, which he was quick to point out. "The bend in the half-pass has to do with the neck," he explains. "For a horse with a very fine neck, if you bend too much you 'break' the neck. If you want more crossing, keep the horse a little straighter. For competition there is only a little bend, because if you have too much, the horse won't cross enough, and they want lots of crossing in competition."

One of the key ingredients of his training of both horses and riders was mastery of the shoulder-in, both on circles and straight lines. "Shoulder-in is a fantastic exercise—with a condition," he stressed time and again. "You must feel the weight on the inside hind leg and not on the outside shoulder."

"Before you start shoulder-in and half-pass, the horse must know how to go forward. I start at about three to three and a half years old, and I start all horses with shoulder-in and after shoulder-in, half-pass."

"Shoulder-in is the 'aspirin' for horses," he maintained. "Every corner is a little moment of shoulder-in. The horse should be bent like a banana."

The Master rides an exemplary half-pass.

After longeing, his young horses usually began work in hand with some little circles in shoulder-in, which he repeated when mounted. Riders were instructed in riding a correct shoulder-in during their first lessons on his schoolmasters, and often learned to introduce it to their own horses via counter shoulder-in during a clinic situation.

"I have never seen a horse give the back before he gives in a lateral sense," Mr. Oliveira was quick to point out. "Put the horse on the bit after the lateral bend."

"If you are able to keep the bend with the inside rein a little lighter than the outside rein—that's very important for collection—you are an intelligent person."

And therein lay part of his genius.

Widely known for his sensitive schooling of fine, hot-blooded horses such as Lusitanos, Anglo-Arabs and Luso-Arab crosses, Mr. Oliveira also schooled a number of Russian horses toward the end of his life. In America, where many students brought Thoroughbreds to be schooled under his tutelage, he was also quick to point out: "I love Thoroughbreds!"

Although he never participated in dressage competitions, he worked with many well-known competitive riders, including Olympic gold medalist Reiner Klimke. Asked about his feelings on competition, Mr. Oliveira replied, "Competition can be very good, because you have a motivation. But when you ride, you must not think about competition, but about the horse. Compete, but don't ride for the competition."

"You American riders are workers," he continued. "You are relaxed in the mind and in the body. I hope that America will truly be a country for dressage, but you must find an American way of dressage. You must stay Americans when you ride, and not try to copy other countries—the Germans, Russians or French—and stay relaxed in the mind."

The Master rides a school trot.

Reflections

"Horses are marvelous," maintained Nuno Oliveira, "more marvelous than we are, and they understand more quickly." He often quoted the French classical maxims, "Calm, forward, straight" and "Ask often, be content with little, reward much."

We lost him much too soon, just at the beginning of the era that would see a schism in the worldwide dressage community, at a time when his knowledge, experience and compassion for the horse were most needed. Regarding the increasing heaviness becoming more prevalent on the dressage scene at the time of his passing, he often lamented: "It is not the fault of the mouth of the horse, but the hands of the rider!"

His influence was truly worldwide. Several Portuguese students of the Master helped with the initial training of horses and riders during the formation of the Andalusian School of Equestrian Art in Spain (now the Royal School) and were instrumental in the founding of the Portuguese School of Equestrian Art. His son Joao lived and taught in America for a number of years, grandson Gonçalo now follows in his father's and grandfather's footsteps, and many other devoted students carry on his legacy in private riding schools around the world.

As he predicted, his true worth is only beginning to be appreciated many years after his death.

Those interested in the teachings and philosophy of this master from Portugal can do no better than to read his own words. Although he published a number of books during his lifetime, eight of which were in English, many of those editions were privately printed and most today remain out of circulation.[10] A volume of his complete works is currently available in French, as well as individual titles, and the German editions of his books are also readily available.

Nuno Oliveira's most well-known book, *Reflections on Equestrian Art,* has gone through several editions and is available in English through many equine booksellers. In the 1988 edition, he concludes this pivotal work with the observation: "Classic and academic equitation is not a spectacle which is lassitudinous [droopy] and dull. It is a calm and serene

---

10 Copies of some of his works in English still appear online, and a new translation of his *Classical Principles of the Art of Training Horses* is currently in preparation.

spectacle in which the horse may be seen to have pleasure....As it may not be well understood, in concluding, I must again emphasise that artistic development obtained by superior techniques must go hand in hand with the rider's tact and feeling, and in the quality of physical and moral decontraction [relaxation] shown by his horse, which makes possible a great interpretation of equestrian art."

Monsieur de Nestier, *écuyer* to Louis XV, riding Le Florido

Chapter 2

IN SEARCH OF THE MASTER

Watching *Mestre* Oliveira schooling his own horses, it is not too difficult to imagine you have stepped back in time several hundred years to one of the small royal riding schools, perhaps even the famous *Ecole de Versailles* itself, where the grand masters perfected their art in the so-called Age of Enlightenment. Certainly the Master's relaxed legs, upright torso with his incredibly strong back, and reins of silk have few counterparts in modern days. It is almost as if a living vision of the old French grand masters on their proud Iberian horses has galloped out of the classic engravings of the time.

To this day, when I see the famous print of Monsieur de Nestier, *écuyer* to King Louis XV of France, I am reminded of an equally famous photo of Nuno Oliveira that has appeared on the cover of a number of modern works. With his tricorn hat and royal blue *casaca* (the Portuguese bullfighter's ornate formal dress coat which most closely resembles the gentlemen riders' frock coats of the 18th century), riding his magnificent grey Andrade Lusitano Euclides in exhibition[11], Mr. Oliveira seems the modern-day model of the old French *maitre.* Indeed, in that same signature coat, but also wearing the historical powdered wig, he is history come alive in an equally famous photo on his bay Ervideira stallion Beau Geste in levade. I strongly suspect *"Le Grand Silencieux,"* as Nestier was called, could never have outshone the modern Portuguese master.

Several notable scholars of equestrian history have commented on Nuno Oliveira's remarkable blending of the Old World with the new. "You do not even have to be a horseman to see the closest semblance to perfection between man and horse when you set eyes on *Mestre* Nuno Oliveira," writes Sylvia Loch in her beautiful book, *The Royal Horse of Europe* (J. A. Allen, 1986). "This great Portuguese classical riding master is acknowledged the world over as probably the most brilliant dressage rider alive. He might well be described as the Guérinière of the twentieth century, and in true Portuguese tradition, he passes on to his worldwide

---

11 See *30 Years with Master Nuno Oliveira* by Michel Henriquet, p. 74 (Xenophon Press, 2011).

Nuno Oliveira schools a young Luso-Arab stallion in piaffe, 1979.

pupils the disciplines laid down by his seventeenth-century predecessor, Marialva. As with all Portuguese teaching, the emphasis is on softness and lightness and this is achieved by a strong active back and seat which give an outward appearance of tremendous stillness in the saddle, for there is no apparent sign of leg and hand aids."

"With his dark, brooding looks, colourful and powerful personality, unmistakable riding figure, and gentle hands," she elaborates in her encyclopedic book *Dressage* (Trafalgar Square Publishing, 1990), "he was undoubtedly the most revered classical horseman of our time. He embodied a last living link with those great classical Masters of seventeenth, eighteenth and nineteenth century Europe. It was not for nought that he himself was called Master by people of every nationality."

Horses for Dressage

Part of Nuno Oliveira's genius, of course, was that he worked with so many different breeds and types of horses and learned astutely from all of them.

"In all types and breeds of horses you can find a good horse for dressage if the horse has good paces and a good mind," he emphasized during our interview in 1978. "A good dressage horse must be round, not too long or short, with a good back—that's very important—and a good neck, good movement, good muscle, and a nice mind. The neck, the back and the croup must be in proportion. Also, the form of the neck is important. But if a horse does not have all of these qualities, you can often transform him. I have trained so many horses with bad necks in my life. You can change a lot of things."

And change horses he did. As a student, part of the fascination, and a learning equally as great as one's own lessons on a privately owned mount or one of his schoolmasters, was the opportunity to spend weeks and months, sometimes years, observing as he patiently changed the horses entrusted to him, little by little, day by day, creating suppleness and movement in horses not particularly endowed with such attributes by nature, and achieving remarkable brilliance with those equine students favored with natural talent.

"A correct mover is more important than a big mover," he maintained, in contrast to the horses often preferred by many modern-day competitors. "Most important, for dressage, a horse must be strong in the back, especially for piaffe and passage."

"Some horses have natural extensions," he continued. "For other horses, with not too much natural extension, you must collect them first for the extension to come from behind. Some horses cannot do a really extended trot, and it's the most stupid thing to force extension without collection."

Ulysses, Portuguese stallion, passage

Above all, according to Nuno Oliveira, "If the horse is light, he must be light in all paces—extended and shortened. The light horse must have much more impulsion. He is light in all his body, not contracted. Impulsion is not hard. If the horse is light, he's much better balanced, because he's relaxed. Light means to have the horse without force."

It is worthwhile at this point to note the esteem in which Nuno Oliveira was held by so many contemporary writers who are well-respected trainers and instructors in their own right. Their moving tributes help us to go far in understanding the man and his enduring mystery.

"Now that Nuno Oliveira has passed away, everybody, even in the official circles of the F.E.I., tends to refer to him as one of the glories of the classical art of dressage," observes Jean-Claude Racinet in *Racinet Explains Baucher* (Xenophon Press, 1997).

In an interview by Hilda Nelson with Michel Henriquet ("Interview with a Grand Master," *Dressage & CT,* September 1994) this esteemed

French student[12], who studied with Nuno Oliveira for over 30 years, put it thus: "Oliveira was for me the greatest intelligence of the century." He goes on to emphasize that "Oliveira had such an open mind, and he succeeded because he also had such a great equestrian culture and was able to make a veritable synthesis between what was most interesting of the *Ecole de Versailles,* that is to say, the idea of the *rassembler* (collection), of lightness and equilibrium, partly obtained through the shoulder-in, and also through use of the pillars, and Baucherism."

"Baucherism," continues Henriquet, "in turn, gave us work in hand. The rider on foot makes the horse execute movements which supple and balance him. What is important is that the horse can move forward, for a man on foot is a living pillar, one who moves forward. The horse is not thrown against the inertia of the pillar. That is what is important. And Oliveira makes a synthesis between the most important aspects of both schools."

Equestrian Culture

To understand the historic significance of this synthesis, it is important to delve into a bit of equestrian culture oneself.

"This 'French-like' horsemanship grafting the Baucherist procedures (lateral and direct flexions of the neck and poll from the ground and, when mounted, at slow paces; maintenance of a permanent yielding of the jaw in action; *'effet d'ensemble'* followed with a total release of the aids; sophistication in the use of the spurs; work in place; importance bestowed upon the movement of rein back...) to the classical progression of La Guérinière (circle, shoulder-in, croup to the wall) is, as it happens, the horsemanship practiced in a very recent past by the unforgettable Portuguese Master, Nuno Oliveira," explains Jean-Claude Racinet in *Another Horsemanship* (Xenophon Press, 1991).

"Then in full possession of his Art," Racinet continues, "Oliveira was first spotted by a group of French riders touring Portugal in the 1950s. Amazed by his *'Maestria,'* they asked, "What kind of horsemanship is this marvelous one that you practice?' And, equally stunned, Oliveira stuttered, 'But...yours, of course; the Traditional French Horsemanship.' "

---

12 See also *30 Years with Master Nuno Oliveira* by Michel Henriquet (Xenophon Press, 2011).

So who was this Portuguese trainer, "a young *écuyer* living in the suburbs of Lisbon who was totally unknown at the time, except for Portuguese horse breeders," as recalled by Michel Henriquet in Hilda Nelson's interview?

Nuno Albreau de Oliveira (1925–1989) was born into what we would today call a middle-class upbringing in the pre-Revolution era when such a background was not so prevalent in Portugal. "What initially separated Oliveira from the majority of his fellow aspirants was perhaps his lack of great wealth," notes Sylvia Loch in *Dressage.* "His family was well-travelled and educated (he had an English grandmother), enjoying responsible posts in the diplomatic service and overseas, but unlike the Andrades and the Veigas, there was no country estate to come to this only son. His father was a banker, and later head of the Lutheran Church in Portugal, and the young Nuno had to make his way in the world as soon as he left school. Fresh from his studies under Portugal's last Master of the Horse, his godfather, *Mestre* Miranda, he set off to earn his living from breaking and schooling horses."

It is interesting to note that at that time (as it still is today at the Spanish Riding School, and a few other places) the equestrian art was passed in a direct line of transmission from master to pupil. There was little confusion, as can result today from the proliferation of books and articles and videos without the filter of expert guidance to help one discriminate.

In his autobiography *Notes and Reminiscences of a Portuguese Rider* (1982) Mr. Oliveira fondly recalls his own training. "I often think back to the time when I began my equestrian career in the riding school of my master, Joaquim Gonzales de Miranda," he writes. "I remember starting to ride on a small Portuguese saddle without stirrups on a horse called Bright, an old three-quarters bred that Mr. Miranda had schooled in dressage as a young horse."

Mestre Miranda[13] served Portugal's last royal family, and as such could trace a lineage of transmission from the acknowledged masters of old. However, he was also inspired by English-born James Fillis, who emigrated to Russia, and had also received instruction from the Frenchman Brunot, among others, bringing a cosmopolitan flavor to the education of

---

13 More details on *Mestre* Miranda's school can be found in Professor Jaime Celestino da Costa's Preface to *30 Years with Master Nuno Oliveira* (Xenophon Press, 2011).

his own students.

Although Nuno Oliveira began his lessons at a very young age, "I was about 12 years old when I started to be seriously interested in equitation," he writes. "There in that riding school, which was a veritable apprenticeship in pragmatic studies, I learned that equitation was an Art, full of subtleties which when practiced would refine all the feelings of the rider for everything that surrounded him."

Of his lessons, Mr. Oliveira recalls: "Mr. Miranda demanded great discipline and perfect calm from his riders, and total obedience. He insisted on absolutely correct movements, so that all his pupils knew how to do every act of high school dressage. Flying changes at the canter were the most brilliant I have ever seen, done in a big stride but having total fluidity at all times, as were the passages which had the greatest suspension I have ever seen, much more than you see nowadays."

Portugal has an incredibly rich cultural tradition when it comes to the equestrian arts. Long before the masters of the Neapolitan School penned their tomes in the Renaissance, the first book on equitation since the Greek general Xenophon appeared in 1434 written by Portugal's King Duarte. Unlike the later Italian masters such as Grisone and some of his pupils, "There is not a trace of cruelty in Duarte's writings," observes Dr. H.L.M. van Schaik (*Misconceptions and Simple Truths in Dressage*, J. A. Allen, 1986).

Jean-Claude Racinet reminisces about his discussions with Nuno Oliveira on the Portuguese riding tradition in his previously cited article "Was Oliveira a Baucherist?"

"He showed me the book from Carlos Manoel de Andrade, *Luz de Liberal e Nobre Arte da Cavallaria* ("Light of the Liberal and Noble Art of Cavalry," 1790). This book, which teaches how to ride 'a la Marialva' encompasses all the aspects of baroque riding and is considered by some as superior to La Guérinière's *Ecole de Cavalerie* (1731) [School of Horsemanship, Part II, Xenophon Press, 1992].

"With their horse, the Lusitano, and this book," observes Racinet, "the Portuguese of the 19th century could have considered themselves self-sufficient. But, as Oliveira explained to me, if politically Portugal was turned toward England, culturally the attraction was toward France. This, added to the natural intellectual curiosity of the Portuguese, led them to be more interested than shocked by the Baucherist reform. The Court of

Portugal sent an emissary to take lessons from Baucher and bring the new method back home. I even remember the name of this emissary, as mentioned by Oliveira: General Luppi."

The question of whether Nuno Oliveira was or was not a Baucherist has been debated in a number of scholarly articles[14] which are beyond the scope of this introduction, and they address the issue in great detail.

"Oliveira managed to interpret the riding of the old school with the innovations of Baucher and other more recent masters and his own personal experience, so that he achieved exceptional brilliance from his horses, with total relaxation and lightness of touch," writes Felipe Graciosa in his book *Escola Portuguesa de Arte Equestre* (Medialivros S.A., 2004).

"So I could see that Oliveira, the undisputed Master of 'classical' riding, was not an anti-Baucherist," concurs Racinet. "Nor was he a Baucherist stricto sensu: he was more than all that; he was the most complete, the most knowledgeable riding Master that ever was."

"The extent of his knowledge and talent," concludes Racinet, "made of Oliveira a man difficult to situate. You came to see the baroque Master, and you met with a Baucherist. But as you just concluded that he was indeed a Baucherist, he showed you that he was deeply involved with the baroque art."

For me, personally, there is little to debate. Nuno Oliveira was— and was not—a Baucherist depending on the horse in front of him at the moment. His genius was that he took from every system and applied it as appropriate, always with the benefit of the particular horse in mind. That was his synthesis, and his selectivity. He refused to be categorized, and we still can't do it today. And that, I think, is his timeless appeal: the best of classicism combined with the best of innovation. His horsemanship was a living, evolving, compassionate work in progress until the day he died.

The Making of a Master

With his impeccable background in equitation, the young Nuno Oliveira set out to acquire the experience that would one day render

14 See Chapter 8, "The Master and 'A Little Baucher.'" See also Michel
  Henriquet's *30 Years with Master Nuno Oliveira,* arguably the most definitive
  work on the subject.

him "the foremost equestrian intelligence of our times, a man of talent, knowledge and passion," in the words of Michel Henriquet (*Henriquet on Dressage*, Trafalgar Square Publishing, 2004).

Fortunately, writes Mr. Oliveira in his autobiography, "it continued to be possible for me to ride after Mr. Miranda's death, due to the fact that at this time cavalry and artillery officers had the right to keep a horse which later they could sell, keeping the profit, and two officers asked me to train their horses. We worked them in the street, occasionally being granted the right to work in the Riding School, which belonged to the military.

"In this fashion I continued on, despite not having a dime in my pocket, until a horse dealer asked me to ride several horses….About a year or so after I started to work for Senor Chefalenez, I was asked by my great friend and student Manuel de Barros to train mares and stallions on the lovely property, Quintas dos Arcos in Azeitao, owned by his brother-in-law, Carlos Riteiro Ferreira. Here I had the opportunity, thanks to a well-built Riding School and horses which I could train calmly, to broaden my

Nuno Oliveira on the Luso-Arab, Tesouro, in collected walk

experience in equitation. In addition, Manuel de Barros had a vast quantity of books on equestrian matters sent from France, which he placed at my disposition."

The rest, of course, is history.

Nuno Oliveira went on to set up his own riding school, Quinta do Chafaris, under the patronage of Julio Borba on the outskirts of Lisbon. Mr. Borba's son Guilherme would train with Oliveira for twelve years, and would be instrumental in founding the Portuguese School of Equestrian Art, serving as its director from 1981–2000. "Nuno does not need any introductions," writes Dr. Borba as quoted in current Director Filipe Graciosa's *Escola Portuguesa de Arte Equestre*, "but I would like to say that, through his pupils and their pupils after them, he and many of his art were behind the foundation of the Portuguese School of Equestrian Art." Many other distinguished Portuguese students also began their careers under Nuno Oliveira's tutelage during this period, and students from all over the world flocked to Portugal after a number of his exhibitions abroad.

Early in his career, Nuno Oliveira exhibited horses he had trained in the international circus at the Coliseu dos Recreios in Lisbon. He showed an Anglo-Arab mare at the International Jumping Show in Lisbon doing an incredible 500 flying changes every stride in a series of figure eights. During a benefit exhibition for the Spanish Riding School in the bullring of Campo Grande he performed an exhibition with Spanish Riding School Director Col. Alois Podhajsky, beginning a friendship which would last many years. In 1962 he exhibited several horses in Geneva, Switzerland, and presented Euclides and Beau Geste at the International Horse Show in Lucerne. His presentation on Euclides in Paris during the Winter Circus was filmed during this era[15]. He also presented horses at the Horse of the Year Show in Wembley, England, and his book *Haute École* was published in England.

During the 1970s Mr. Oliveira also began giving lessons to the riders of the Cadre Noir in Saumur at the request of his friend, then Lt. Col. Pierre Durand (former Commander-in-Chief of the Cadre Noir). He taught officers at the Mafra Military School near his home, and he also taught regularly in Belgium for many years[16].

15 Film footage of the time is included in the DVD *Nuno Oliveira*, a film by Laurent Desprez (24 images, 2009).

16 For detailed notes from these teachings, see *The Wisdom of Master Nuno Oliveira* by Antoine de Coux (Xenophon Press, 2012).

In 1972, he gave his first clinic in the United States, and in 1973, a year before the Portuguese Revolution, he built the stables at Quinta do Brejo in Avessada, where he lived and taught until his death during a clinic in Australia in 1989, where he died peacefully in his sleep.

Words of Wisdom

"In all the world I tell my students the same thing," Mr. Oliveira reiterated during one of our last interviews. "The hands must follow the back. It is when riders forget this that they create problems in the horse. Push your stomach and back forward and keep the rein for a moment, a fraction of a second. Take and give with the fingers. If you don't relax after a second, the horse resists."

Dr Guilherme Borba, student of Nuno Oliveira, first director of the Portuguese School of Equestrian Art

"Use the right action in the right moment. Don't stay an hour doing the same thing. And don't go in a straight line all the time, but work circles, shoulder-in, halts, etc."

He constantly cautioned riders to be aware of the effect of their position on the horse. "Don't put the leg too far back," he warned. "Legs too far back make the horse's hind legs contract. Relax the legs. You ask impulsion not only by your legs, but by your seat. Use your seat to help the horse. If your legs are too strong and push all the time, they don't push the horse forward, they contract him. When you contract and press with the legs you contract your back and can't use your seat. The horse stays tight, not relaxed and engaged."

Lightness of the rein aids was definitely a hallmark of his teachings. "Use small vibrations on the reins when you need them," he instructed. "Play the piano with your fingers. If the horse resists on one hand, you must play with that hand. When the horse gives, the rider gives. Resist in the right moment, then relax."

Legendary Lightness

This legendary lightness, both in his own riding and his best students, presupposed an erect, classical position with what we would today describe as a strong core. "Do some half-halts by your stomach and back," he advised. "Your hands must follow your back. If you forget you have a back and use only your hands, the horse puts the head down but does nothing behind. And if your reins are too short or too long, you cannot use your back."

"Take with your back very gently and stay light with your hands. Push the back forward and shut the fingers when he resists, and open the fingers when the horse relaxes. Give immediately when the horse's weight comes back. Close and open the fingers. That's very important till the end of the life of the horse."

In a nutshell, his teaching was deceptively simple: "Relax the hands, yet keep the contact. Horses don't need strong hands. You use your aids, and when you feel the moment the horse gives in any exercise, you give – your hands and also your legs—and the horse stays in position, but not by force. Riders have a tendency to forget this," he reminded his students again and again.

Nuno Oliveira was uncompromising in his beliefs. In the copy of a manuscript he gave me of a work describing his teachings shortly before his death, he penned this dedication in French for his students (translation is mine):

"A man. . . is one who is tranquil with his conscience even if the crowd is in disagreement. It is after his death that one sees what was not true in what he made."

For those who accept his philosophy and make it their own by truly practicing it in their own riding and teaching, Nuno Oliveira's equitation still remains the truth.

Nuno Oliveira and Tesouro, piaffe

A modern-day Alter Real stallion

Chapter 3

NUNO OLIVEIRA, LIGHTNESS, AND A LOVE AFFAIR
WITH THE IBERIAN HORSE

"Horse breeding owes a great debt of gratitude to Nuno Oliveira, of which few are aware," writes Filipe Graciosa in his marvelous book, *Escola Portuguesa de Arte Equestre.* "Oliveira was, without a shadow of a doubt, the Portuguese horseman with the greatest international projection."

This high praise from the second director of the Portuguese School of Equestrian Art is founded on a rich history. In the previous chapter we discussed Mr. Oliveira's philosophy and his early background which led him to espouse the precepts of lightness that would become his hallmark in the 20th century.

**Riders of the Portuguese School of Equestrian Art
performing at Queluz Palace, Lisbon, Portugal**

With his breathtaking Portuguese stallions Nuno Oliveira burst upon the international scene like a shooting star in the 1960s seemingly from out of nowhere, and his light has never been eclipsed.

"By teaching and exhibiting a number of Alter Real stallions (Farsista, Curioso, Corsario, Ansioso, Farsola, Soante, etc.) at home and abroad," observes Filipe Graciosa, "Nuno Oliveira demonstrated that the Alter Real horse still had untapped potential for development and, of course, for improvement."

We have already discussed his "discovery" in the 1950s by a small number of French writers and trainers who quickly realized his unique worth and began to spread the word beyond Portugal's borders.

In 1958 a French businessman, August Baumeister, purchased a Lusitano from the Andrade stud that was in training with Mr. Oliveira. A few years later he shipped the grey Lusitano, along with a Lipizzaner who had also been in training, to Switzerland. The Lusitano was named Euclides, and in 1962 an international star was born when Nuno Oliveira and the beautiful young stallion performed an exhibition on the day of the Grand Prix at Lucerne which was filmed for Eurovision.

Footage from a 1963 exhibition in Geneva shows the pair in the most brilliant, majestic passage imaginable. While many observers have commented on the height of the passage and the regularity of the footfalls, for me it is the perfect, unvarying cadence of the young Euclides which shines through, even with the less sophisticated video technology of the day.

Shortly after his wildly successful exhibitions in Switzerland, Mr. Oliveira was invited to show Euclides in Paris at the Winter Circus during the benefit, *Gala de la Piste*. "I had never ridden Euclides on a circus floor before," he recounts in his autobiography, "but he performed splendidly, executing, amongst other movements, perfect flying changes every stride, and pirouettes."

To fully appreciate the difficulty of this feat, one has only to watch film footage from this era, as the circus flooring was installed in a circle certainly no more than 13-15 meters, so all exercises had to be performed on this small circular track. In a video from Mr. Oliveira's exhibition on Euclides at the *Gala de la Piste* in 1966 I counted 37 flying changes at every stride performed on this circle, almost all of them jumping through with an engagement and agility one rarely encounters on circus flooring, followed by his brilliant passage and then a transition into a beautifully round, fluid, elastic Spanish walk such as one rarely sees anywhere, on any footing.

"When it is said by certain riders who think they are great classicists that circus riding is of no value, I laugh," observes Nuno Oliveira of his Paris exhibitions and his performances as part of an international circus at the *Coliseu dos Recreios*.

Worldwide Acclaim

"Of course, the choice of a horse must first be a love affair," advises Nuno Oliveira in his book *Horses and Their Riders* (Howley and Russell, 1988).

It is impossible to discuss the artistry of the Master without giving tribute to the instruments of his artistry, his beloved horses. Although he loved sensitive horses of all breeds, it is with the horse of the Iberian Peninsula he will forever be linked, and his work with the baroque horses of Portugal garnered worldwide acclaim not only for his horsemanship but also for the Lusitano.

"In every breed of horse, one finds both good and bad horses. Some breeds have a greater number of horses which are more appropriate for one thing or another," he continues. "But in all breeds one finds good qualities of gaits, balance and strength among many individuals."

"Of course, due to its conformation, being high at its withers and to its great lateral suppleness, the Iberian horse is more apt to stay on its haunches and to turn on a shorter base than most breeds," observes Oliveira.

"The extensions of the gaits are less pronounced in the Iberian horse than in some other breeds. However, there are some Iberian horses that do have good extensions."

Due to his artistry and his great technique in enhancing his horses' natural movement, Mr. Oliveira was able to cross boundaries in the horse world as easily as his exhibition horses crossed European borders.

Alter stallion, piaffe between the pillars

"The school [Portuguese School of Equestrian Art] exists thanks to Oliveira."

Dr. Filipe Graciosa interview Nuno Oliveira (*24 images, 2009*)

33

Performing with Colonel Podhajsky

A truly historic performance occurred during a benefit exhibition of the Spanish Riding School of Vienna, performing in the bullring of the Campo Grande. Colonel Alois Podhajsky, the legendary Spanish Riding School director, rode his famous Lipizzaner Pluto Theodorosta, and Nuno Oliveira rode Garoto, who later became one of his schoolmasters after retiring from public performances.

"It was late in the afternoon when the Colonel was mounted, and I was asked to follow him into the arena," recalls Mr. Oliveira in his memoirs. "Out of a corner of my eye I watched him and executed every movement with Garoto which he did on his horse. For a half an hour we continued in this fashion, and the Colonel was very admiring of my horse's ability. Afterwards, we were introduced formally to each other by my great friend Fernando Sommer d'Andrade. I said how much of an honor I had felt it to be to have had the pleasure to see his equitation, and he replied politely that he had much appreciated mine. We then became fast friends, and five years later when I went to Vienna he gave me a marvelous welcome, extending his hospitality outside of the riding school."

The importance of Mr. Oliveira's influence on the modern Alter Real and the Portuguese School of Equestrian Art has already been mentioned. In light of this, it is worth telling the story of his beloved Alter stallion Corsario. "I remember that after my father's funeral," writes Mr. Oliveira, "I returned to school starting to work Corsario on the lunge exactly as I always did. He stopped and put both ears forward, looking at me; an exceptionally sensitive horse, he felt that my state of mind was not as usual, although everything else was the same as it had always been." Corsario, he concludes, "was the most beloved of my horses due to his temperamental character and his extraordinary beauty."

In addition to performing benefit exhibitions for the Alter stud, he also showed two Alter horses, Curioso and Ansioso, at the Horse of the Year Show at Wembley in England, helping win friends for the breed overseas. "Oliveira had given some very impressive demonstrations at Wembley and in Rome with his Lusitano stallions in the days when, to many equestrians, dressage meant little more than indoor riding," recalls Sylvia Loch in *The Classical Rider* (J. A. Allen, 1997). "What set him aside from other contenders was the absolute controlled power of his horse while he himself appeared to do nothing. To the undiscerning, it was as though he merely sat there, very still with motionless legs and reins of silk. They could not fathom it out. People still talk about the moment when Oliveira, unmoving, impregnable as a rock, made his finale and cantered backwards in front of the Royal Box at Wembley. The control was unreal."

Beau Geste, Lusitano stallion in passage

Collection

Today, people exposed only to modern competitive dressage still have trouble fathoming it. So foreign has this level of collection become in our modern day that many people have never seen it, and so have no basis for comparison.

In the films I possess of his beautiful bays from those early years I am struck time and again by their remarkable impulsion, lightness and mobility. I think particularly of an incredible ride performed in the privacy of his small arena. With reins in his left hand, whip held aloft in the style of the Old Masters during their exhibitions as proof of the lightness and submission of the finished high school horse, Mr. Oliveira gives a breathtaking performance of lateral mobility including canter half-passes and flying changes, repeated half pirouettes *(passades)* toward the wall, impeccable transitions into piaffe, and from piaffe to canter, as well as incredible vertical impulsion demonstrated in *terre-à-terre*, *mézair*, canter in place, canter backwards to forward canter, haunches in and shoulder-in during canter on the circle, and multiple levades.

The canter pirouettes done toward the wall from just a few meters away are spectacular, his mount moving unerringly, seemingly under his weight alone, hand and leg aids barely perceptible. The pirouette in piaffe is equally brilliant with its collection and absolute mobility. As a whole, the performance is truly astounding.

Breathtaking Artistry

This ride alone is a ten-minute exposition of the axiom "forward." I am particularly impressed as the most difficult airs and transitions are all ridden one-handed with a degree of suppleness impossible to believe if one has not schooled and exhibited horses oneself with all four reins in one hand. (For reasons I will mention later, Mr. Oliveira once insisted I school my Grand Prix horse in the pirouettes and flying changes every stride with the reins in one hand. This is an incredibly difficult feat—I am not talking about exhibiting a finished horse, but actually training the movements with one hand—and when I watch his old films I am inspired anew with the artistry he achieved.)

Indeed, so many fine horses from Portugal's great Lusitano stud farms honed their art under Nuno Oliveira's tutelage that it is hard to choose a favorite among them. Certainly the Andrade stallion Euclides is probably the most famous, but the bay Alters and the beautiful grey Zurito of Veiga bloodlines instantly come to mind, as well as a host of other pure and crossbred Lusitanos who formed the ideal of the classical horse so long ago that still dances undiminished in my mind's eye.

I possess films showing some of these horses, in various exhibitions, demonstrating brilliant counter changes in half-pass in passage with impeccable rhythm, and brilliantly forward flying changes. Exhibitions in long lines exhibit the same remarkable impulsion, whether in piaffe, canter in place, or *mézair* leading to lovely rounded *ballotades*. Even when cantering backward, or performing repeated levades, it is obvious from these films that the Master's horses are always thinking forward!

I don't think it is an exaggeration to say that Nuno Oliveira put the classic Lusitano on the worldwide map at a time when it was little known outside Portugal. When I look at my lovely three-year-old Lusitano standing in my barn—of mixed Veiga/Andrade lineage, distant cousin to some of the Master's horses—and at all the lovely Iberian horses of my students, I am reminded of his living legacy to the world every day. Certainly the first time I experienced the heaven to be found on the soft but powerfully flexing back of a truly light, fully collected Lusitano was on his horses, and when it came time to start my first young Spanish horse under saddle I was truly fortunate to have his guidance, for the sensitivity of the Iberian horse has to be experienced to be believed.

The Iberian Horse

"It is necessary to delve a little into history in order to appreciate our present day and to understand a little the basic fundamentals of Equestrian Art and its evolution," observes Mr. Oliveira in *Classical Principles of the Art of Training Horses* (Howley and Russell, 1983).

Spain was a great power and conquered a large part of the world thanks in great measure to the mobility of their horses, according to Nuno Oliveira.

"When the horsemen came from the north of Europe, mounted on large and heavy horses with heavy armor, they were defeated by the

Spanish cavalry. Not only were the Spanish horses lighter, but much more mobile, and capable of outflanking the others and turning in all directions. This resulted in a desire to give to other types of horses in Europe the same mobility as the Genet of Spain." As history shows, the equestrian academies founded in Naples led to the proliferation of training for the high school airs in the Renaissance, not always by the gentlest of means. Oliveira points out that the Frenchman Antoine de Pluvinel studied at the Neapolitan school and brought the teachings of the Italian masters back to France, albeit with a gentler touch.

"He was the first Frenchman to have the title *L'Ecuyer* and was the teacher of King Louis XIII," he states. "With Louis XIV, the most celebrated Equestrian Academy in the world, the School of Versailles, began. The horses which the Masters used with most pleasure were the Spanish breed."

French Classicism Returns Home

It would be impossible to leave the brief highlights of Mr. Oliveira's long and illustrious career without mentioning his work at France's Cadre Noir. Following one of his exhibitions with Euclides at the *Gala de la Piste* in Paris, he was invited by then Captain Pierre Durand (later Commander-in-Chief of the Cadre Noir) to present Euclides at Fontainebleau before the Cavalry officers. Although unable to accept the invitation at the time, he invited Captain Durand to ride Euclides. "Durand rode him brilliantly," recalls Oliveira, "and exclaimed emotionally, 'He goes perfectly on to the bit. This is the horse for the Commander-in-Chief of the Cadre Noir!' "

The two remained friends, keeping up a steady correspondence, and in 1978 Nuno Oliveira traveled to Saumur to teach from his extensive knowledge of French classicism for several days at the Cadre Noir. Later, on one of his first visits to Saumur in several years, he trained a horse in piaffer for his old friend, then Commander-in-Chief.

In the book *Long Reining* (A & C Black, 1992), Philippe Karl, former member of the Cadre Noir and instructor at *l'Ecole Nationale d'Equitation*, observes, "In one of those lapidary passages of which he was such a master, Maestro Oliveira said: 'There are two things in riding: technique and the soul.' "

Nuno Oliveira's soul shines through his simple yet brilliant writings again and again. In the chapter "The *Ecuyer*, Teacher and Trainer" in *Classical Principles of the Art of Training Horses* he offers these priceless gems:

"The true *Ecuyer* is not limited by any system or any rules. He must know that different roads lead to Rome.

"The *Ecuyer* is the one who has trained many horses, the one who has spent hours and years on the back of horses, meditating and thinking and enriching his knowledge, and being capable of transmitting all his knowledge.

"The *Ecuyer*, who is growing old and losing his physical capabilities, knows how to appreciate those of his colleagues or younger students and is the one who will be pleased if, one day, one of his students, due to his teaching, will have superior equestrian qualities of his own.

"The *Ecuyer* is the one who knows how to remain humble and who, through his professional honesty, will know to make his student a friend."

Nuno Oliveira succeeded in transmitting much of his technical expertise to students around the world through the years. Sadly, near the end of his life, he remarked that too small a number of his many students around the world truly "got it" in terms of the heart and soul of his riding. But the quest goes on.

Teachings on Lightness

"The difficulty in dressage training is the mobilization of the horse, a gymnastic exercise which must be done in an ordered manner, without haste, as otherwise it results in nothing," cautions Mr. Oliveira in *Reflections on Equestrian Art.* "If these gymnastics are done methodically, without haste, a great degree of mobility may be obtained; a mobility which will bring impulsion and lightness in its wake. Afterwards, the rest is simple.

"The most complicated airs of dressage are not difficult if they are tried on a mobile, light horse."

Farther on, he reminds us that in addition to calmness, lightness, and submission, which are desirable in all exercises, there must also be added constant impulsion.

It is this unparalleled blending of calmness and lightness with almost unbelievable impulsion and mobility which gave Mr. Oliveira's exhibitions such brilliance.

Today we live in an era where many true horse lovers long for a return to the lightness and ease personified by the old French classical traditions as taught by Nuno Oliveira.

If you have followed the Xenophon Press series of books on Nuno Oliveira thus far, you are probably such a seeker. Those of you who may have been privileged to know Nuno Oliveira personally, or to study with him or one of his students, are probably feeling nostalgic and even a bit bereft. Despite his wishes quoted earlier, we must acknowledge there has been no young maestro, no new genius like the young Nuno Oliveira, to supplant him.

Over the years, I have found I can do no better than return to the Master's words, for there we find a real guiding light and an inspiration that never disappoints.

Whenever I encounter a difficulty with a horse, or find myself at a loss with a particular student, I take myself back to Mr. Oliveira's clinics or my days in Portugal. In my mind's eye I walk again the dusty track from the rural village of Avessada, strolling past donkey carts, past cows being driven to water, up and down the picturesque Portuguese hills on the way to the Master's arena. On my way I may encounter a groom leading a beautiful Lusitano to the farm, or a donkey set loose to graze. Once I have set the scene in such a meditative moment, an appropriate quote usually comes to mind. I remember the Master's deep, relaxing tone of voice, his immovable calm, and I know that with knowledge, time and patience, a solution always comes.

Our next chapter features specific suggestions for various dressage exercises and movements taken from Mr. Oliveira's lessons, along with his suggestions for correcting common problems and achieving the lightness we seek.

For now, I would like to end his tribute to the baroque horses of Spain and Portugal with the closing words from his own memoirs:

"Today...I am sitting in my hotel in Brisbane, Australia, where I'm giving lessons for two months as well as riding two horses, writing all this down not because of personal vanity but because I want to speak of the Iberian horse.

"Here I ride an Andalusian, called Amarillo, a young horse. Obviously, as a horse grows older he grows physically more apt to develop his work into art, enlarging the spirit and thought put into it. When I see the progress of the boy I am training here, and of the other two students I feel that my time has not been wasted and that I can still transmit much of my hardly acquired knowledge and experience which, in this vast world, equates to love."

Tesouro, half pirouette at canter

Zarco, Portuguese stallion, passage

Chapter 4

SCHOOLING WITH THE MASTER

If someone were to ask me, "What is the greatest piece of advice you ever received from Nuno Oliveira?" I would probably answer with the quote we mentioned in the last chapter that "the most complicated airs of dressage are not difficult if they are tried on a mobile, light horse."

It is achieving this lightness and mobility that is the never-ending quest. If we also adhere to his philosophical ideals of kindness, love and respect for our horses, then the methods used to achieve these goals are equally important.

Not surprisingly, paging through my notes from many clinics over the years shows repeated, equal emphasis on these maxims with horses and riders of all types.

With a green horse, insists Mr. Oliveira, "First put the horse forward! Don't let the horse sleep. Use a working trot, not a sleeping trot. The rider must know what is his horse's trot and do all things to maintain that trot. The hind legs must push all the body of the horse forward."

"Look to your cadence in all work," he reminded riders constantly. "Don't forget cadence, especially when you think of impulsion. Good impulsion is when you feel the horse come up from the ground with a good vibration, with a good position of the head and neck. The horse is capable of keeping the same cadence and power without your hands and your legs. I don't say loosen the rein, but keep a soft contact. If you need to do things constantly with the legs and the hands, the horse is not really in impulsion. He must carry it himself, and the back and mind of the rider hold."

Also for green horses, "Come to a walk only after a good trot," he advises. "If you ask for correct transitions and halts, if the horse does not have enough impulsion you can spoil the impulsion. When I ride a horse I do halts in the beginning. With most riders I don't ask too early because they are not capable of putting the horse forward."

It is definitely worth noting here that Mr. Oliveira sought lightness in his horses and his students' horses from the beginning. He upheld the French emphasis on lightness of the jaw, schooling his young horses in a simple snaffle and a classic dropped noseband if needed. He did not like the flash noseband, considering it too restrictive, and often had new students at a clinic remove it. (The even more restrictive crank noseband had not yet invaded the scene.) We still lived in an era when a horse lightly chewing his bit(s) was a desirable feature of the soft, classically trained horse, who went with a politely adjusted noseband, or sometimes no noseband at all.

The less restrictive equipment with which we rode under Mr. Oliveira's tutelage, of course, contributed to the necessity of developing light, educated hands. "I cannot control my rage when I hear it said that the horse must be permanently pressed against the bit as this is the only way to vary the speed as wished, and the only way to have a completely straight horse," he laments in *Reflections on Equestrian Art.*

He was always quick to point out that there should be no confusion between this heavy tension on the bit and the necessary light contact which activates the reins. He was adamant that, while results may be achieved by pushing the horse hard against the bit using a methodical gymnastic program, better results may be obtained by relaxing the aids (*descente de main*).

As others have observed, being trained by a true classicist can be both a blessing and a curse. The beauty of such training, especially if one has both feeling and a keen eye, is that one has been exposed to the highest standards of the art, which are simply considered routine in such a venue.

The difficulty is also that one has been exposed to the highest standards, etc.—which means that one is not easily impressed, and can become a bit disillusioned when lowered standards become touted as the norm.

Since Mr. Oliveira's death, I am sure most of us who knew and admired him have been wondering how his legacy would unfold. I had not written any new articles on his work for many years until *Horses for Life* magazine suggested reprinting these interviews as I, along with many others, had been waiting for someone far more qualified to pen the definitive study of the Master and his work.

In the meantime, I agree that it is past time to introduce Nuno Oliveira to the current generation of riders who may have heard his name and been curious about his work, but perhaps frustrated to find most of his own books out of print. Thanks to Xenophon Press and the recently translated works by two of Mr. Oliveira's longtime students, Michel Henriquet and Antoine de Coux, we now have not one, but two serious in-depth studies in English of the man and his methods.

It is in the spirit of education we offer this third short work. Mr. Oliveira's advice which follows is taken from many years of quotes from my personal notes. I have left his comments as pithy, and with the same charming syntax, as he delivered them in the hopes that reading the cadence of his own manner of expression might give you the feeling of having your own moments with the Master.

Nuno Oliveira, extended trot on the purebred Arab Valioso

Notes from Nuno Oliveira's Lessons

Some General Guidelines

Ride with discipline, not force.

Discipline is very important. A circle must be round, not like an egg or a potato.

Use the corners. Each corner is a moment of shoulder-in. If the rider goes into the corner, the horse is more obedient, more engaged, and easier to ride.

Any time a horse makes a mistake in an exercise, start again from the same point.

Never finish any exercise with the horse in resistance.

Keep contact with relaxed hands. Use small vibrations on the reins when you need them. When a horse resists on one hand, you must play with that hand.

Transitions

When asking for a halt, advance the stomach and brace the back.

In transitions to and from trot, with your shoulders back, push your stomach forward and then, by your back, trot. Don't take the reins.

Do some half-halts by your stomach and back.

Keep the horse straight and push.

Go more easily to departures, rein back, etc. Pay attention to halts and departures, but use less force. Relax.

Shoulder-In

Shoulder-in is like aspirin for horses. Use shoulder-in to supple and engage the horse.

The body of the horse must be bent like a banana. Keep the quarters near the wall and don't break the neck or you put the horse's weight on the outside shoulder. You must take both shoulders in and feel the weight on the inside hind leg.

The quarters must push, not follow the forehand.

Keep your own shoulders back and bend the horse around your inside leg, but not too far back. Ask the shoulder-in by the leg, not by the rein. If he resists, use a supple inside rein. Play with it.

Play piano with your fingers.

Half-pass

The horse's shoulders should be slightly advanced. The rider's inside leg is important initially and in the last few steps.

You send the horse with the outside leg and receive it with the inside leg. Don't put the outside leg too far back.

When first teaching half-pass, don't ask too much bend. Ask only two or three steps in the beginning.

If the horse tilts his head, use the opposite rein momentarily.

Canter

Every horse has his own canter, and the degree of collection in canter depends on the degree of collection already achieved in trot.

On straight lines, the horse must be straight. If the horse always canters with the head bent too much to the inside, later he will have trouble with straight flying changes.

The flying change must be 'flying' and straight. The quality of the flying change depends not on how strongly you touch, but on the quality of the first canter.

The secret of the flying change is bounce in the canter. Ask more power in the canter and confirm the first aids for one or two strides before asking the flying change. Keep the head and neck straight, make sure the horse is round, then 'fly' through the change.

Dressage means fire in the saddle, fire on the rider's bottom!

Piaffer and Passage

It is the fault of most riders that in teaching the piaffer they ask too much and upset the horse. You must have patience and ask only a little.

The reason so many horses are not able to do a brilliant passage is that the riders work too many steps at first. Too much passage with a young horse can confuse the trot work and lead to a lazy passage when the horse is older.

Piaffer is easy with a lot of sugar!

Nuno Oliveira rides Ulysses in passage, reins in one hand, after two years' training.

Chapter 5

"FLYING" THROUGH THE CHANGES

WITH NUNO OLIVEIRA

Some of the most intense and long-lasting technical advice I gleaned from the Master over many years involved riding, training, and later teaching, flying changes.

My introduction to Nuno Oliveira had come at a fortuitous time in my education. I was a fairly experienced rider at the time, comfortable fox hunting, eventing at the lower levels, and starting my own young horses, but had not yet received training in advanced dressage, so there was fortunately not too much for my mentor to undo.

Except, that is, when it came to flying changes.

Changes ridden at the forward canter or gallop required while negotiating jumping courses are a practical matter, ridden by necessity in a more horizontal balance than the flying changes we look for in dressage. As such, if the horse stiffens slightly during the change, loses his balance momentarily or changes without being completely straight, it is sometimes overlooked.

Such bad habits can become ingrained, of course, and will certainly compromise work on sequential changes in the future for a dressage horse, so it's much more productive to learn the changes correctly from the start.

"Some horses quickly become calm and straight during flying changes without altering the canter's rhythm," writes Mr. Oliveira in *Reflections on Equestrian Art*. "Others have great difficulty when this exercise is demanded.

"Each rider having enough tact and enough patience, while repudiating violence, can obtain flying changes quickly in the first case.

"In the second, the problem must be resolved by great masters as it is one which takes a lot of time."

I was extremely fortunate to have that great master to teach me how to resolve the difficulties with a horse in the second category, and so I hope his advice will prove useful to others struggling with sequential flying changes, one of those rites of passage into the loftier realms of dressage.

Canter Prerequisites

"It is necessary to make a complete study of strike-offs at the canter, practicing them from the walk and from halts in order to completely understand and execute correct flying changes," counsels Mr. Oliveira in *Reflections*. Flying changes should not be started, he continues, until the horse is calm in the canter and can easily strike off from the walk, remaining straight, in either direction. The horse must also be able to maintain a balanced counter canter.

I had brought my event horse, Raindrop, who also doubled as one of my dressage horses at the time, to my first clinic with Mr. Oliveira. Although his canter work was quite good for the dressage tests we were then riding, it quickly became apparent that he was struggling in the small 15 x 30 meter arena where we were attempting to maintain a straight, balanced counter canter. His solution, as we careened a little too quickly through the corner and my weight shifted slightly, was to offer a flying change, which I of course had provoked.

The Master was not impressed.

We worked a lot in that clinic on walk to canter and walk to counter canter transitions, interspersed with quiet halts, slow rein backs, and then a straight depart into canter or counter canter. By the end of the clinic we were both much better balanced counter cantering through the corners and around a 15 meter circle, and in fact Raindrop's canter was so much improved that he won his class at the East Coast Regional Dressage Finals the next day and even emerged with the high score of the show.

While this was certainly gratifying, what impressed me much more was the powerful collected canter I was beginning to feel as a result of these simple canter exercises. Watching Mr. Oliveira school flying changes on another student's horse was also a revelation.

In his memoirs, Mr. Oliveira recalls his own mentor, *Mestre Miranda*, achieving the most brilliant flying changes he had ever seen, ridden in a big canter stride but with total fluidity.

In that clinic, I began to be introduced to how the brilliance of the old classical teachers becomes handed down in an almost sacred tradition, and I was blown away with the work I saw that week, especially some of the brilliant flying changes.

When Mr. Oliveira gave the students their homework until the next clinic, to which I was invited, I was not surprised that strengthening Raindrop's collected canter was high on the list. And, he asserted, with a finality that brooked no argument, "You come to Portugal before the spring!"

And so it was arranged. The fact that I was young and on a tight budget did not matter. Much to my surprise and unending gratitude, I had been given a three-week scholarship, lodging included, and I was off to ride with the Master. To this day, I think Raindrop and I amused him. I'm sure he saw no great talent that week, but merely a sensitive, forward-going horse, a somewhat fit rider with a fairly decent seat and leg position, and an interesting challenge: exactly how far could he teach a rider with only one hand to train her own horses?

Changes (including Canter) in Portugal

I have described the Master's school in Portugal in detail, the atmosphere and the school horses, in an earlier chapter. While I loved all the work I experienced during that first trip, it was the training in canter I found most productive at that time. I was given several school horses who did really good flying changes, including the one-tempi changes, and probably was schooled through more flying changes in those first three weeks than I had ever ridden in my life.

What made the experience especially interesting, in addition to the impeccable schooling of the horses, was that I was learning to ride four-in-one at the same time.

At home, when I rode in a snaffle, I used a custom designed rein with a set of loops of various adjustments on my left arm, in place of the missing hand. When I rode in a double bridle, as I sometimes did fox hunting or showing in sidesaddle appointments classes, I rode three-in-one: left snaffle only on the left, right snaffle and both curb reins in my right hand. This had served me well over the years.

Mr. Oliveira did not particularly like this arrangement. He wanted me to ride with all four reins in one hand; after all, he often checked the schooling of his horses by performing movements with one hand, and also did many of his exhibitions the same way, so who was I to question his wisdom? It did, however, add an interesting dimension to learning to ride some of the advanced movements at the same time, particularly the tempi changes.

Today, looking back, I realize he was correcting a tendency I had developed to stiffen and drop my left shoulder and take my elbow forward, which could have become a significant problem, but at the time adjusting to riding four-in-one was a real challenge.

My hot little chestnut schoolmaster made life especially interesting at the canter. Transitions, collected canter, and counter canter on the circles progressed well. Even shoulder-in and haunches in on the circle at canter were not too difficult once I figured out the extra flexibility required in my wrist and elbow riding four-in-one. The first few flying changes went well. I was delighted; I had never felt such powerful, uphill changes before, and keeping my horse straight was proving easier than I had expected riding four-in-one. But suddenly, as commands for the changes increased in frequency, I found myself flying around the little indoor school, almost totally out of control. My leg aids for the flying changes were obviously stronger than this hot little stallion thought polite; as we charged around the arena in a really forward medium canter, I inadvertently shifted my weight as I attempted to regain some collection and control, and suddenly we were flipping two-time changes straight up the long side.

"Control your horse!" instructed Mr. Oliveira calmly as we passed him on the fly, still flipping flying changes I wasn't intentionally asking for every few strides. If it is possible to be both exhilarated and mortified at the same time, I certainly was.

Once I relaxed my legs and kept my seat quietly where it belonged, my little stallion settled back into the loftiest collected canter imaginable: brilliantly forward and uphill, yet light as a feather. Mr. Oliveira sent us through a few more flying changes in the same canter, and I was hooked.

I think I was laughing when we stopped, and he was smiling as well. "He is an old horse," he commented, "but he is a fine horse. You pushed too much!"

And so I learned from my fiery little chestnut one of the great secrets of flying changes: prepare the canter with the right degrees of impulsion, straightness and collection, and the changes will almost take care of themselves. With the right preparation it is only necessary to ask the change softly and then allow.

It is obtaining the right canter for each horse that is the art.

Pearls of Wisdom

In my first few months of riding with Nuno Oliveira I learned that he usually didn't say much, but that what he did say was golden. A few sentences could contain the most important keys to progression through the often labyrinthine levels of dressage.

His writings are the same: often deceptively simple, they lay out the template of progressive training for those with the sensitivity to appreciate them, and also with enough experience to realize that the secrets are all there.

As a young trainer, nowhere did I find this more applicable than with the preparation for training flying changes.

"During canter departures the horse should elevate his forehand rather than throwing himself forward," he reminds us in his memoirs. "The rider should not try to put the canter in cadence if the horse is not collected, otherwise there is a risk of loss of impulsion. Obviously, the more the canter is slowed down, (ultimately the canter in place) the more impulsion is needed.

"In order to have a nice rocking type canter instead of a forced flattened out one, the horse must be straight, so try not to over-bend him, avoiding the use of the inside rein as much as possible, and conserve the cadence by placing the horse's shoulders properly. In this pace, the outside rein serves to set the horse back on his haunches while the inside rein elongates and lowers the neck."

Above all, he reminded us constantly, a flying change is really just a canter departure. In order to obtain good flying changes, the canter on each hand must be made as perfect as possible. The changes should be asked for calmly and there should be no visible effort on the rider's part as he asks for them.

One great secret, he explained, is to be sure that the shoulders of the horse are aligned exactly with the hindquarters, as many riders make the mistake of trying to do flying changes with the haunches in. It is much better to do two good flying changes rather than a number of poor ones, he cautioned. "Remember that it is of primary importance to have the form of the canter correct before any changes are asked for, and increasing the intensity of the aids will not help unless the canter is good," he reiterates in his memoirs.

Riding Mr. Oliveira's schoolmasters had drilled these points home, and by the time I left Portugal after my first trip I had begun to develop the kinesthetic memory for the correct preparation and flying changes on the trained horse. I was also beginning to understand that the canter required to ride a single change differed from the canter for sequential changes every four or three strides, and that differed yet again from the two-time changes and the flying changes every stride. And it was different with each schoolmaster I rode.

The question was whether I would be able to apply this knowledge, and my newfound feel, to training my own horses when I returned home. It was time to put it all to the test.

A Generous Horse

Every so often as riders we are graced with a really generous horse which, while it may not have the greatest conformation or movement compared to some other horses, is blessed with what experienced horsemen often call "heart," for want of a better term.

My beautiful Raindrop was such a horse.

We continued jumping for a while, which he enjoyed, but it was time to specialize, and I knew I wanted to take him as far as Mr. Oliveira thought we could go. I had bought an off-the-track Thoroughbred that someone had tried to make into a hunter rather too quickly and I needed help with this rather nervous horse as well, so I decided to alternate both horses at the clinics.

The Thoroughbred's rehab went rather simply. Mr. Oliveira had us do a lot of bending and stretching, and we worked a lot on lateral flexions in the walk and trot. Since he wanted me to do these one-handed in the snaffle as well, even on my greenie, I became more adept handling the reins in such a manner and applied my more educated hand to Rain, whose program also included a lot of lateral work at the walk. With horses like Raindrop, the quality of the canter depends on the walk, he explained, and we worked constantly on developing his suppleness with a lot of shoulder-in and half circles executed in haunches in, which began to lead to lovely walk pirouettes.

Before tackling the flying changes, Mr. Oliveira wanted us comfortable schooling in a double bridle. We introduced it during a clinic under his supervision, and all went with no problems. A bold horse, Raindrop had no tendency to over-flex, and I had really worked on developing a light, educated hand in Portugal, so introducing the double brought us a new level of lightness and subtlety.

We introduced a little piaffe in hand to strengthen his back and hindquarters and increase collection. To further strengthen him, and also to develop shoulder mobility, Mr. Oliveira had us ride a lot of transitions between shoulder-in and haunches in at collected canter on the 15 meter circle. We introduced the half-pass in canter as well as canter to halt transitions, and under his watchful eye Raindrop was transformed into a powerful yet light, upwardly mobile dressage horse. Here his genius finally became apparent to me, as I found it much easier to keep my shoulders parallel with my horse riding one-handed, and so made it easier for Raindrop to find his balance while learning these movements.

Finally, it was time to teach the flying changes Mr. Oliveira's way.

Introducing the Changes

We introduced the changes the way Mr. Oliveira usually began. Once the collected canter was quite nice—for Raindrop, this was best achieved with a lot of transitions, interspersed with halt, rein back, and haunches in on the circle—we were instructed to go on a large circle at one end of the arena. Keeping the canter light and cadenced we were told to take the long side, paying special attention to straightness. At the other end of the arena we were to walk, go on a large circle, then take the long side and ask frequent transitions from walk to counter canter to walk. After passing the first corner at the end of the long side in counter canter we began a large circle in counter canter, did a transition to walk while still on the circle and at the beginning of the next long side did a transition to counter canter. After a few steps in this collected counter canter, we were to walk and come back to the same place in the arena several times and ask for a new transition to counter canter.

We were then told to go onto a circle in canter on the true lead at the end of the *manège* before the place we had been asking the counter canter departures and go very deeply into the corner. At the spot where we had been doing the counter canter transitions, keeping the inside shoulder back I was told to momentarily tighten the fingers without pulling and then give a very quick, light, electric touch with my inside leg (which would then become the new outside leg if we achieved the flying change from the true lead to counter canter).

If the first flying change happened as requested, we were to halt quietly after several steps of counter canter and reward with a walk on the long rein. After this short break we were to return to the same end of the arena, do a transition into the true canter as before and calmly pass the same place we had asked the flying change, this time without asking the change.

This method worked beautifully for Raindrop and me. Not only did changing from true canter to counter canter keep us straight in the change, it also developed huge amplitude in the change while preserving balance and calmness.

It had the added advantage that for a horse like Raindrop, used to changing leads with each change of direction while jumping, he learned to wait calmly for the aids and not to anticipate the changes.

"So many times I have seen a horse ready to give his first flying change easily," writes Mr. Oliveira in *Classical Principles of the Art of Training Horses* (Howley and Russell, 1983), "and his rider instead of asking with tact (care) has given the aids too strongly so that the horse remembers and remains excited each time that he thinks one is going to ask for a flying change, or, as with certain horses, they remain for a long time nervous each time they pass the place where the demand was made." Mr. Oliveira's seemingly unorthodox method of introducing the changes as described above nicely circumvented the problem of nervousness before the flying change, as well as producing really beautiful changes.

When working at canter, all of us were advised not to shorten the canter until the horse had developed enough muscular strength. "Don't use too much inside rein," he constantly corrected. "If you do, the horse puts weight in the shoulders." He also warned that with too much inside rein in counter canter, "you put the quarters out and lose the mechanics of the canter." He advised us to keep the horse's head straight in counter canter, and also to keep the neck straight in the flying changes.

Freely Forward

"In canter, the rider must feel the horse bounce," insisted Mr. Oliveira. "Make sure the canter is good—bounce!—and then 'fly' through the change," he instructed, making sure to keep the horse's weight on the hindquarters.

During our early change work, it became apparent that Raindrop had an easier time jumping through from left to right. Outdoors at home we worked on developing what I came to think of as our "power" canter: very forward, very engaged and very uphill on an extremely light rein. Mr. Oliveira explained that it can be helpful when a horse has difficulties to aid him with a light seat in the changes. This was balm to my ears, and we practiced changing a lot from right to left, both on the long side, through the short side and even on circles, with me in almost a half seat until both changes showed the same engagement, throughness, and length of stride.

I remembered watching the Master school three-time changes, two's, and even one-tempi changes in the same light seat on some horses not yet fully developed, and I suspected that would be part of our program later when we progressed that far.

Once we were straight before, during, and after the single change on both reins, first from true canter to counter canter, and then from counter canter to true canter, we were allowed to progress to the next step, asking two successive changes. I was always careful when schooling changes at home to have a ground person. It is not always easy to feel if a horse is a hair late behind, but a good ground person can alert you instantly if it should ever occur in order to prevent the development of this bad habit. Our single changes, therefore, were calm, clean, and quite respectable, with anywhere from four to six single changes now interspersed somewhere in the middle of the ride, but I wanted to wait to introduce successive changes under the Master's knowing eye.

We began with two flying changes on the long side. Mr. Oliveira wanted us to begin with the change to counter canter at the beginning of the long side. I chose to begin tracking right, so that our first change was to left counter canter. This went well, and so toward the end of the long side, after no particular number of strides, but when Raindrop felt straight and balanced and ready, I was to ask the second change, this time from counter canter to true canter on the right lead.

Ah, success again, punctuated with the Master's "very nice." I was instructed to return to walk and to reward. We began again on the left rein. Our left canter didn't feel quite as cadenced to me, but Raindrop was straight and willing, and I decided to go for it. The change to right counter canter at the beginning of the long side was certainly "flying," and I had a momentary flashback of galloping past the Master in Portugal several years before, flipping leads out of control. I relaxed, asked Raindrop to come back to me, which he did very politely, but he was one smart horse and I knew he was anticipating the second change at the end of the long side. Game on—we "flew" through the change to the left—and although I was delighted with his willingness, Mr. Oliveira was not satisfied. "No," he corrected. "The horse was not straight." He worked us awhile in walk to canter transitions and canter to walk, interspersed with left shoulder-in at the walk and some left circles at both walk and canter, and after a few minutes the corrections succeeded and Raindrop offered the second change in the corner from right to left in a manner that met with the teacher's approval.

When working in the more powerful canter, he suggested, I could begin to reduce the canter one or two strides before the change to the left. "Do not let the horse go!" he cautioned. "Do one or two times a halt."

58

With this attention to detail, we were soon ready to reverse the order of the changes, now going from counter canter to true canter at the beginning of the long side, and from true canter to counter canter at the end. With this preparation, he then considered us ready to begin on the diagonals.

At about this stage I really began to get a feel for how important it is to take a lot of time and patience in developing the flying changes, even if the horse is eager as Raindrop was and seems able to do more.

"Now is the time, if one is a purist and wishes to continue," he writes in *Classical Principles*, "that the horse is now ready to bring the changes closer together. Before beginning the timed flying changes, it is necessary to do single changes on the short side, on the circles in both directions and on both reins." The progression must be slow, he cautioned, and when beginning the changes between a certain number of strides, it is important during the strides between the two flying changes to reinforce the aids of the canter with each step to confirm the lead on which the horse is already cantering, reversing the aids at the precise moment of the second flying change.

The other point he reiterated is that you need a certain degree of collection for flying changes every four strides; for the three-time changes you need a slight increase in the degree of collection, for the two-time changes a little more, and so on, with the one-time changes requiring the utmost collection.

Putting It All Together

Always adhering to Mr. Oliveira's advice, and with his help during his regular clinics every few months, over the next few years Raindrop developed lovely sequential changes. I always waited to start the next series under his eye, and although I did all the riding and training myself—he never rode the horse except once, at the very end of Raindrop's schooling purely as a favor, so I could have the joy of watching him ride my beloved horse—if we succeeded in achieving good changes it was purely due to Raindrop's generous heart and the Master's expertise and inspiration. Like most young trainers learning to school the sequential flying changes for the first time, in the early stages I felt I was really sometimes just along for the ride.

During this time I had the opportunity to put the changes on several other horses as well. I found if I paid meticulous attention to Mr. Oliveira's progression, I could usually stay out of trouble.

"This is a subject with enormous importance," he reminds us in *From an Old Master Trainer to Young Trainers* (Howley & Russell, 1986). "You do not have one system for all the horses." For some horses, he observed, you must ask the first changes in a more shortened and "sitting" canter, others in a larger and less collected canter.

"Not to know in which canter you must ask the first flying change of a horse is a fault of observation, of reflection, and sometimes ignorance," he writes.

"Certain horses stay easily in a more large canter and they stay more balanced and calm. To those horses you must ask the first flying change in that canter and confirm in that canter.

"Also start the timed flying changes in this canter and when they are confirmed then start to reduce the canter and you must know until what point you can reduce the canter so that the flying changes stay flowing forwards."

Raindrop had certainly been such a case, and I often found myself returning to our "power" canter throughout his training. It was interesting when I encountered the opposite type of horse, one not able to stay balanced in the more forward canter at first, and I learned to collect the canter quite a bit more, as he advised, while paying attention to absolute calmness before preparing for the first changes.

Aside from Mr. Oliveira's schoolmasters, it was Raindrop who taught me the most about training flying changes, and for me his changes remain my standard of feel to this day.

The day finally came, not too long after we had confirmed the two-time changes at a clinic with the Master's nod of approval, that it was time to tackle flying changes every stride.

By now we were comfortable doing two-time changes on long, straight lines and around circles. I think Raindrop, who was in his prime, really enjoyed showing them off, and they were tremendous fun to ride.

60

Our instruction, as with all of the previous series, was very methodical. Mr. Oliveira explains the method in *Classical Principles*, and we followed it to the letter: "On a long side, put the horse at the canter, either true or counter canter. It is necessary to think beforehand which is the easier flying change, the one right to left or the one left to right, for all horses have a side which is easier. If your horse, for example, is easier in the flying change from the right to the left, you put him on the track to the right rein in counter canter, with attention to maintaining the impulsion and collection and the position absolutely straight. You give him the aid of flying change from counter canter to true and, while this flying change is not yet completed, you ask him the opposite aid from true to counter canter. It is necessary that your legs be perfectly free and relaxed to be able to act quickly and without harshness. Now the horse has given two flying changes in one time. Reward him on a long rein and, if you feel it necessary, work him a little at a collected walk before asking him the same on the other side. When he has done what you asked, dismount and send him back to the stable."

While it may seem too good to be true, Raindrop passed this hurdle fairly easily thanks to Mr. Oliveira's excellent preparation.

The rest of our progression also went literally according to the book. We continued for a few days to ask these two flying changes alternating sometimes from true to counter canter, or from counter canter to true canter, continuing the same slow progression until we could obtain the two one-time changes in an easy manner on both reins. We were then instructed to move to schooling three flying changes in the same manner, spending even more time than with the previous changes. When a horse does this easily and calmly you can ask for four flying changes, observed Mr. Oliveira, and only when he has given four flying changes easily is he ready to increase the number of steps. "Here it is of course, also necessary to go progressively and do not finish the lesson with flying changes in one time, but after the one time flying changes reward him adequately with walk on long reins and finish by flying changes in two time," he writes.

The greatest difficulty we encountered during those times was finishing with the changes every two strides. About this time I asked Mr. Oliveira if I might return occasionally to schooling three-in-one. He thought about it a long time, watched me ride some changes that way, and agreed. I suppose he felt he had corrected my left side well enough by then, and the three-in-one sometimes gave me that extra edge in finishing with straight flying changes every two strides.

I will never forget the day we confirmed the flying changes every stride. I showed Mr. Oliveira the series of three and then four one-tempi flying changes we had worked hard to develop at home. "Yes," he said each time as we cantered by.

Emboldened, I looked over to the corner where he sat, smoking as always his ubiquitous cigarette. "We're not finished yet," I replied as we came through the corner by his box in counter canter, Raindrop maintaining really nice impulsion and cadence. At home, we had gotten up to six or seven nice one-tempi changes, and Raindrop felt wonderful that day, so I decided to risk it. I think I asked for five or six flying changes every stride, but Raindrop felt so good I must have lost count. I think we finished with seven or eight. I had never been so proud of my horse.

Mr. Oliveira said not a word as I dismounted and left the arena. I was a bit despondent. The changes had felt really good, and I was wondering where my feel had gone awry.

Fortunately, my husband came to help untack and congratulated us on the changes. "But Nuno didn't like them," I replied. He looked at me strangely and laughed. "Don't you know he was wiping away a few tears when you finished?" he asked. "That's why he didn't say anything."

I remained doubtful until the Master met me at the barn door a little while later. He handed me a copy of the new edition of one of his books, and took my arm to escort me to the reception being held in his honor.

Later, over a welcome glass of wine, I peeked inside the book. Beside the frontispiece he had written, in a bold flourish, "To Stephanie, with my admiration for the brilliant flying changes of your horse. Love, Nuno Oliveira"

It is one of my fondest memories of the Master.

**Stephanie Millham with Nuno
Oliveira**

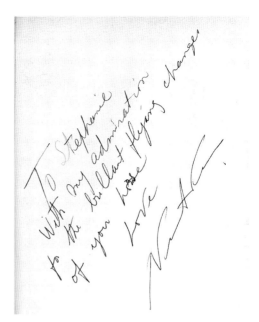

**"To Stephanie
With my admiration for the
brilliant flying changes of your
horse. Love, Nuno Oliveira"**

Schooling tempi changes the Master's way on Raindrop

Nuno Oliveira with Listao in long reins, canter in place after six years' training.

Chapter 6

THE ART OF THE *HAUTE ÉCOLE*

After approximately six years of regular work under the Master, Raindrop was consistently schooling all the Grand Prix movements, though at that point I did not consider them polished enough to show in a dressage test.

"When a horse knows all the movements of Grand Prix they never forget," Mr. Oliveira told me. "Now you conserve, correct, and polish little things."

During a clinic shortly after we confirmed the flying changes every stride, we began concentrating on perfecting the quality of the piaffe and passage, and especially the transitions between them.

Arguably the most beautiful airs of high school dressage to many people are the piaffe and passage when performed classically, with true lightness and collection. Nuno Oliveira was renowned worldwide for the brilliance he produced with countless horses in these airs, often with horses with no particular talent for them. There is, in fact, an old joke that refers to a well-known competitor who, when asked what to do with a horse that wouldn't piaffe, replied: "Put him on a train to Nuno."

Though humorous, the answer is justified. Watching Mr. Oliveira school piaffe and passage over many years with horses of all breeds was akin to studying for a master's degree in the various techniques to achieve these high airs. I think the reason why so many onlookers appeared mystified by how easily he made the most ordinary of horses dance beneath him is that they had missed the painstaking preparation in the simple, basic exercises that allowed the piaffe and passage almost to fall into his lap with such seeming ease.

When asked which air to begin first, his answer was always, "It depends." With a fairly quiet horse, but one with good impulsion, he suggested starting with the piaffe first.

Since this was the case with Raindrop, we worked the piaffe initially. As I had by then observed the work in hand carefully for a number of years, and introduced the lateral work, halts and rein back in this fashion, Raindrop learned the piaffe as the Master usually taught it: work in hand. Of course, the technique had to be modified for us slightly, since I had only half a left arm and thus needed to stand much closer to my horse than is usual for the work in hand, but the principle was the same: with the horse straight along the wall, stand by his inside shoulder, inside rein held close to the snaffle, outside rein crossing the neck near the withers, and held along with the whip in the other hand.

From this position Mr. Oliveira had us work a lot of halts followed by immediate transitions to trot, then halt, gradually reducing the number of strides of trot between each transition, until Raindrop began to "fall" into the first half steps of piaffe. Always he emphasized the importance of keeping the horse rigorously straight in this exercise, and I soon found that even a slight deviation from straightness, with a shoulder-in or haunches in I had not asked for, meant we couldn't do it.

"Use piaffe as an exercise to put the weight back," he instructed us time and again. When Raindrop did not lower his quarters sufficiently—after all, he was built in a more horizontal balance than the typical Iberian or modern warmblood—we were to rein back calmly between transitions. These repeated exercises soon had him light and mobile, attentive and without tension.

One of the big secrets, he emphasized, was to do only a little, and to stop while the horse was still willing to offer more steps. We were also to continue to advance slightly, rather than ask for a piaffe in place.

Finally, as I concentrated on animating Raindrop during this careful work in hand, Mr. Oliveira reminded me seriously: "Stephanie, it is the horse to do piaffe, not you."

In this way, the piaffe began to develop a lovely rhythm. A slow, high piaffe is not in the range of all horses, cautioned the Master, and it is important not to ask more in this movement than the horse can do.

He also cautioned us to make sure the walk stays absolutely calm during the schooling for piaffe and not to lose our calm, immobile halt, which can sometimes happen during the schooling for piaffe.

This method worked beautifully for Raindrop, and the piaffe under saddle progressed along the same lines. "Some horses must return to the same place" when schooling the piaffe, he observed; "others must advance to a new place." Raindrop stayed equally relaxed either way. Mr. Oliveira then cautioned that in the mounted piaffe, it is important to finish the exercise with a quiet halt or walk on long reins, and not to introduce the idea of a difficult transition (such as a forward trot or canter) out of the piaffe too soon.

When this stage had been achieved, we were instructed to go forward out of the piaffe in a shortened collected trot, paying attention to the lightness and collection with impulsion. As this school trot became really confirmed, with light alternating leg aids we were to begin adding a few strides with slightly more suspension which over time began to develop into the cadence of the passage.

Once again, instructed Mr. Oliveira, the secret was to ask only a few strides at a time. When Raindrop wanted to offer longer steps, in a more horizontal balance, we were instructed to keep the steps short and slow, paying attention to the cadence and collection and not to allow the seemingly more spectacular steps. Only when the collection in the passage was confirmed, and we began to marry transitions between the piaffe and passage, could we begin to vary the length of the steps.

Although I had ridden these transitions many times on a number of Mr. Oliveira's schoolmasters, in teaching Raindrop I found the transition from piaffe to passage much easier than the reverse.

Mr. Oliveira instructed me to ask the transition after only a few steps while the passage was still very collected, with good suspension and weight on the hindquarters, and to be careful not to block with the hand. "Keep the horse straight," he reminded me. The increase of collection in the transition, he instructed, must be achieved by the rider's back and not by the reins, which must remain very light. Unlike the tempi changes, where I had been advised to lean a little forward in the beginning to make it easier for my horse, in this transition he cautioned me not to do so, but to sit especially straight and aligned, though still relaxed. We struggled with the transition for a while, often losing either the cadence or the collection, until a remark he made to another rider also solved the difficulty for me.

For some horses, the Master explained, you think of the piaffe as a passage on the spot. When I thought in those terms and tried again, we finally managed the right balance and impulsion for a seamless transition. As Raindrop became stronger over time, it was a real joy to ride circles and even half pass in the passage, done as Mr. Oliveira instructed by the framing of the light leg aids rather than much guidance with the reins. Although he possessed no particular natural talent for these airs, Raindrop became incredibly soft and light in both thanks to Mr. Oliveira's insistence on "ask often, be content with little, reward immediately."

With other horses possessing more talent for collection or with a more nervous temperament, both traits found in some Iberians, he often proceeded differently, beginning first with passage. The piaffe must be achieved by calming this type of horse, he insisted, not exciting him. What is important for all horses, he explained, is that the collected school trot must be really confirmed in lightness and impulsion before starting the high airs.

68

We were encouraged over time to seek to bring out all the brilliance the horse was capable of, but also to recognize and never go beyond each horse's limits.

Canter Pirouettes

About the time we were polishing the piaffe and passage, we began seriously preparing for the full canter pirouettes. Mr. Oliveira explained that the added strength and collection Raindrop had achieved, especially from the piaffe work, would make possible a much more seated collected canter, or "pirouette canter." We had already schooled some half pirouettes with him, where he had us take a diagonal in counter canter and ride the half pirouette toward the wall before reaching the first quarter line, all in the same energetic canter we did the tempi changes.

It was now time, he instructed, to develop much more power and collection in the canter. He achieved this with Raindrop by putting us through a series of repeated transitions rather than staying in canter for long periods of time. We could already do walk–canter and canter–walk transitions easily, but he now asked us to ride canter–halt, halt–canter, canter–halt then rein back–canter just as proficiently and calmly. Calmness was not our issue in these transitions, but at first straightness was. As Raindrop became comfortable with the increased level of collection and stayed straight throughout, Mr. Oliveira had us ride some steps of piaffe followed immediately by a walk pirouette with a transition directly to canter and a half pirouette in the same collection. He alternated these transitions by putting us on a small circle in collected canter and sending us directly from shoulder-in to haunches in to shoulder-in repeatedly until Raindrop was not only forward and upwardly mobile in his collected canter, but extremely maneuverable with the lightest of aids.

We were then ready to begin to reduce the collected canter while going straight to almost a canter in place, with the same cadence and lightness, ridden almost entirely with aids of the back and light leg aids. He explained, and I quickly found out, that the reduction in the canter stride requires much more impulsion. I actually found it easier to keep the collection and straightness one-handed in these exercises than I had in the tempi changes and the passage–piaffe transitions. Mr. Oliveira explained that very often riders will bend the neck too much in the canter, which makes it hard for the horse to elevate his forehand every stride, and that if one uses too much hand in the pirouettes the horse will begin to bob up and down with the head and neck. It is important, he stressed, that the horse enter and leave the pirouette in the same rhythmic canter, and that the pirouette itself be ridden with the *descente de main* (release of the hand).

Work above the Ground

During the time we were working on much higher levels of collection, I approached Mr. Oliveira one day with a query. "I am interested in levade," I told him. Did he think Raindrop was strong enough to learn this air?

Mr. Oliveira had us warm up in hand. He had us work shoulder-in, some halts and rein back, then piaffe, all the while saying not a word. Then he came down from his box and asked if he might work my horse in hand a little.

He went through the same exercises, Raindrop working well, although he had never been worked by the Master. Mr. Oliveira asked several short sessions of piaffe, each time increasing the impulsion and engagement, rewarding lavishly at each increased effort. During the third repetition, while in a highly collected piaffe on the spot, he placed his whip gently just above Raindrop's hocks, gave a small vibration on the curb, and Raindrop lifted himself into a levade.

He rewarded, allowed Raindrop to stand quietly, then asked another piaffe and a second levade. Again he rewarded, asked a quiet halt, and handed me back the reins.

The Master then gave me the greatest lesson, and probably the greatest gift, I ever received from him. "You love the horse," he told me quietly. "His eye tells me he is not happy with levade. So we do not do levade with this horse.

"It is not interesting to do movements in resistance."

Over the years I have tried to apply this valuable philosophy to my horses and students, always with good results. Later, in a different clinic with Mr. Oliveira, I would learn that horses will sometimes offer one of the vertical airs as an evasion when asked for more collection than their strength allows. But that is for the next chapter.

Nuno Oliveira on Beau Geste, Lusitano stallion, levade

Nuno Oliveira works a young stallion on the center line with meticulous attention to straightness and suppleness.

Chapter 7

THE MASTER AS THERAPIST

Lameness, according to Nuno Oliveira, is often caused by working horses with a hollow back. This observation, made over a quarter century ago, goes along with the latest findings on equine biomechanics[9].

"There is only one equitation—good or bad," the Master maintained.

"Riders start to oblige the horse to do exercises before they put the horse in relaxation," he explained. "When I ride a horse I don't do the movements to show. I am working exercises to work the body of the horse in relaxation. Every time you ask the body of the horse an exercise he must be capable because he is relaxed."

This insistence on relaxation was the reason, he explained, he was able to achieve the beginning of advanced movements such as passage and flying changes every stride so easily. "Others spend years because they force," he observed.

"If the horse is not relaxed, he is not in a position to receive anything."

This relaxation, when coupled with the superior impulsion he achieved, produced remarkable brilliance in horses of all types.

"Quickly pass from one exercise to another—that's the secret to have the horse forward," he instructed. "Don't have the false idea you need to go in big movements to have the horse forward.

"Dressage is when the weight stays in back. When the weight

---

9   For further study, and the benefits of the kind of walk lateral work advocated by Nuno Oliveira, see *Balancing Act, The Horse in Sport–An Irreconcilable Conflict?* by Dr. Gerd Heuschmann (Trafalgar Square, 2012).

comes in front, the horse is not forward."

"Never ask things if the horse is heavy. The most important thing is to prepare the horse to do this or that."

"When a horse does something very good, drop the reins or do some rising trot. Have the horse fresh."

Chewing the bit, he maintained, is a sign not only of relaxation in the mouth, but relaxed neck muscles as well. "Too tight a noseband, and also too tight a curb chain, the horse is too down and strong," he warned.

Some difficult horses, he explained, he might work only at walk for some time.

"Dressage begins and ends with shoulder-in," he repeated time and again. "Riders have the idea to work walk to trot to canter. Use a mixture of movements, and apply every movement in the right moment."

Specific exercises were chosen to remedy different horses' contractions and loss of balance. "Halt and rein back lots of times, not one and then another a half hour later," he told one rider. "Repeat exercises to bring the weight back."

For another rider with a more advanced horse, "Use piaffe as an exercise to put the weight back," he suggested.

The roundness and correct use of the horse's back muscles was emphasized again and again. In addition to the use of lateral flexion and shoulder-in addressed earlier, Mr. Oliveira made frequent use of stretching in his clinics. Some off-the-track Thoroughbreds were asked to trot with good impulsion in a long and low position, neck extended with the nose close to the ground, for quite some time to strengthen the back and allow the horse to begin to lift and carry the rider.[10]

----

10 See *The Wisdom of Master Nuno Oliveira* by Antoine de Coux (Xenophon Press, 2012), Chapter 11, "The Young Horse," for an in-depth presentation on this technique.

One such Thoroughbred I took to Mr. Oliveira for rehabilitation was kept in this long and low frame for months to remake his back muscles after years on the racetrack. Mr. Oliveira instructed us not to canter during this period, as this horse was far too excitable, but to intersperse periods of the stretching trot with lots of slow walk work in circles, shoulder-in, haunches in and later half-pass. We were also told to do lots of halts on a loose rein with extended head and neck. After two clinics, and the homework ridden in-between in this fashion, this very hot horse became remarkably calm and strong.

Another horse I took to him received a different suggestion. I was having trouble balancing and strengthening a young Andalusian mare I had started who, despite careful longeing, breaking-in and conditioning, was not progressing very well. A state-of-the-art veterinary hospital we were referred to could find nothing wrong with her, but I knew she was not right and wanted Mr. Oliveira's opinion.

On day one he watched her longe, work in hand, and do some simple walk, trot, and canter work. Though obedient and very willing, the mare was obviously nervous and struggling with the simple exercises—some big circles and straight lines, and a little beginning shoulder-in at walk. On day two, Mr. Oliveira took the mare from me to work in hand. He worked her about ten minutes in a slow walk with some halts, rein back and a little shoulder-in. Then he had me ride a little walk and trot, and watched attentively as we cantered a circle, took the diagonal and attempted our first easy counter canter. "Keep the neck straight," he cautioned as we counter cantered through the first corner, lost our balance in the second corner, and came back to trot on the long side. I dismounted, happy he had seen enough and did not ask us to repeat the exercise. The mare had felt so wobbly I was concerned she might trip and fall. "I know I have a problem," I told him. "Can you tell where it is?"

I will never forget the honesty of his reply.

"I don't know," he told me. "But I think it is in the back."

He suggested I longe and work the mare in hand only for a while to see if she improved. She did not, and retired early as a broodmare. Today, with the prevalence of EPM and other neurological diseases, I am certain she could have been diagnosed and effectively treated, but this was before that era. However, I remain impressed to this day that the Master identified the area of the problem when a number of veterinarians had not, and he did not offer false hope that it would be fixed with further training.

Like the Thoroughbred, my third rehab with the Master ended quite happily. My old friend Raindrop had slipped on a patch of ice and taken a fall, injuring his left shoulder. Once fully recovered from the injury and back in work, it was obvious that while there was no residual lameness or gait abnormality, there was significant atrophy to the infraspinatus muscle and he no longer possessed the shoulder freedom that had made his passage and extended trot so expressive.

Mr. Oliveira had us ride a lot of the suppling walk lateral work, and repeat it in a soft school trot. We did a lot of shoulder-in and haunches in on the circle, and not too many half-passes. I had played around before with teaching Raindrop a little Spanish walk in hand just for fun, and Mr. Oliveira suggested some mounted Spanish walk could be therapeutic for the shoulders.

We began with the easy side first, two or three steps with the right foreleg only, placed on the inside, and staying rigorously straight along the wall. Raindrop picked this up easily, as he had already done it in hand, and was soon offering several nice steps, straight and relaxed with a lovely round back and a beautiful lift in the right shoulder.

The left side was not so easy. Mr. Oliveira allowed us to figure it out, rather than coming down into the arena to help us from the ground. I could keep Raindrop straight fairly easily while riding with just the snaffle rein in one hand, but even when I strapped a dressage whip to my left arm to allow me to touch his shoulder, Raindrop had a lot of trouble lifting and extending the left leg. We persevered, only a few steps at a time with lots of rewards, and over the months the

Nuno Oliveira with Ulysses, Spanish walk

exercise did its job. The Master was right; Spanish walk had been wonderfully therapeutic for Raindrop's shoulder. Sometime later, he was able to lift and extend the left foreleg with the same freedom as the right when we married the two sides together, and his passage and extended trot showed no difference in the diagonals.

When questioned why he taught the so-called circus airs of Spanish walk and Spanish trot, Mr. Oliveira always touted their therapeutic value for some horses provided they are ridden calmly and correctly with a rounded back.

At the end of Raindrop's schooling under Mr. Oliveira we even played with a little bit of Spanish trot. The Master cautioned that this air should be attempted only with a horse with good hocks, which Raindrop fortunately possessed. He had us develop the first steps from a passage, once again on the easy right side first. When we moved to the harder left side, the Master chose to assist us from the ground. He had us ride a small circle around him in passage and asked Raindrop to lift and extend the left foreleg with a touch of the whip as we returned to the long side. This worked after several repetitions, but that diagonal was never as easy, and I later decided not to take the Spanish trot any further. The exercises had been of immense therapeutic value, and I did not want to overdo them to the point of becoming stressful.

In all my years of working with the Master he only suggested one exercise I politely declined, and this happened quite by accident. The first time he ever came out into the arena to assist me with schooling the passage, Raindrop was not quite sure how he felt about having the Master beside him with a long whip as we passaged up the long side. Mr. Oliveira tapped lightly several times in the rhythm of the passage to increase our collection and animation. Raindrop reacted by sitting down and leaping one impressive capriole. "Don't be worried," the Master told me with what I am sure would have been a gleam in his eye if I could have seen it while we were airborne. "We teach this horse capriole!"

"No," I replied when we returned to earth, "no, we do not!" My back was already beginning to feel the aftereffects of years of earlier falls, and I instantly decided Raindrop's talent for capriole would remain forever unrealized. Mr. Oliveira took our refusal with grace, but I still remember the glee in his voice as we flew through the air above his head.

Riding with the Master was certainly never dull.

Notes from Nuno Oliveira's Lessons

(The following notes were taken from some of Mr. Oliveira's lessons that I observed with horses with specific problems. The quotes are similar to quotes in several of his books, with some slight variations for different horses and riders, as he repeated many of the same instructions to his students worldwide over the years. Once again, I have left the cadence of his words exactly as he spoke them.)

Do things in the right moment.

Don't block with the hand. Take and give.

Take and give within a fraction of a second.

The art of riding is for humans to learn to be as quick as horses. Horses are much more quick than us.

Do all lateral movements in the same short walk.

A relaxed shoulder-in is the most important thing.

Stephanie Millham leads the ride on a Luso-Arab schoolmaster, free walk across the diagonal, at Quinta do Brejo.

Don't wait for God to send you the shoulder-in.

Before shoulder-in don't start without good cadence. Put the horse in a circle and see if there is good contact on the outside rein.

Use the outside leg to bring the outside shoulder in.

If the head is in the air, put the horse on a circle, put the hands apart and play with the reins.

From shoulder-in return to the circle with the head down.

When the horse gives inside in shoulder-in, then the head comes down not by force in trot.

Shoulder-in until the horse gives, then straight. Keep both reins the same length when you go straight. Keep your hands quiet.

Trot immediately after shoulder-in. The horse must go BOOM.

Rising trot, and when good, then bring the hand up and sit a few steps.

Keep your whip by the quarters.

Don't let the horse sleep.

Going Forward

The horse must go forward. Use your back, then your seat, then your leg, then your spur, then the whip, and if that doesn't work use the atom bomb.

In every horse you must know the degree, and also the degree is different in different moments of his training.

Shoulder-in to quarters in—it's a dance, not rigid.

Don't let the horse shorten the trot in the shoulder-in.

Don't do half-passes until you have a good shoulder-in on that side.

A big fault is riders start to have too much bend in the beginning.

In half-pass your shoulders must be parallel to the horse's shoulders. Keep the inside rein near the neck of the horse. If you need to make a correction during half-pass use the outside rein. When you have difficulty with the half-pass, open the outside rein.

Open the outside rein when the quarters don't move over in half-pass. Bend the horse to the inside and use outside aids. Keep your weight in the center.

Keep the same contact in both reins in half-pass. Use more inside leg so the shoulders don't move too quickly.

Don't have more contact in the inside rein than the outside; otherwise you pull him onto that shoulder.

Rider Position

Keep your arms next to your body and don't trot with your hands. Every part of the rider's body must go to the floor relaxed.

Keep the shoulders back. Feel your stomach moving up to your chest. In canter, push your bottom forward. Relax your back and keep your bottom in the saddle.

Don't press the legs. If you press the legs the rider contracts the back and also the horse.

Use the legs not too far back, especially in lateral work.

If the horse is heavy—overbent and down—play with the reins. Keep the hands up until he is relaxed.

Don't surprise your horse with your hands when you change from movement to movement.

If the horse resists, extension is not the exercise to do. Put the horse light.

Don't break the neck of the horse. Hands separated to stabilize the base of the neck.

Insist, but not by force.

Discipline—take a straight diagonal.

Change the position of the rein if the horse resists. Don't block. Move the hands until the horse takes the right position.

Don't block with the hand. Take and give.

At halt, very gentle vibrations for grinding teeth.

Keep the neck straight in the canter–walk simple changes.

Keep the neck of the horse straight in counter canter.

Use the outside leg for the canter depart. Don't shorten the canter until the horse has the muscle. Don't use too much inside rein. If you do, the horse puts weight in the shoulder. Too much inside rein in counter canter, you put the quarters out and lose the mechanics of canter.

Flying Changes

Preparation for the flying change: canter a circle, cross the diagonal, change the bend of the neck and counter canter with the head bent to the inside of the *manège.*

Get enough impulsion before the change. Shorten the canter with the outside rein before the flying change.

After the first flying change, now pass in counter canter.

Flying change too fast puts weight to the front. Shorten the canter for one or two steps. On the change from right to left, keep the right shoulder back; take the right rein. Shorten with outside rein and push more at the same time to get more power in the canter.

A horse needs much more power in flying changes every stride. Flying changes every stride is a different movement.

Keep the cadence. When the horse is too fast, he puts weight in the shoulders.

Every horse has his own cadence. When the horse is in his cadence, the trot is easier, more relaxed, the head in a better position.

If the head is in the air, put the horse on a circle, put your hands apart and play with the reins.

Halt with the back and relax the reins.

Sometimes go to the center. With long reins do a small circle. Bend, with the head down. Use more leg than hand till the horse gives inside.

Trot, halt, do a slow rein back, then quickly forward. If you go too quickly back, and too slow to the front, the horse doesn't engage the hind legs.

Piaffe

Piaffe: Touch with the whip on the lower haunch under the buttocks for hind leg animation, above the tail for rhythm. Touch on the leg to lift higher. Touch on the chest for animation and height.

The big secret to do piaffe is after some steps stop and let the horse think.

In piaffer, alternate the legs for cadence. Use the legs at the same time for more elevation.

In passage, don't move the legs too much.

Don't work all the movements your horse knows every day.

Equestrian art begins with the perfection of simple things. We are serious riders here, not jokers.

Nuno Oliveira works on lightness in passage with a Lusitano stallion.

Chapter 8

THE MASTER AND "A LITTLE BAUCHER"

We come now to one of the most complicated, but perhaps most important, discussions involving Nuno Oliveira's work:

Was he or was he not a "Baucherist," a true follower of the innovative French trainer François Baucher? This question has probably sparked more heated debate in the highest circles of equestrian literature than any other aspect of the Master's work. I submit that the question as posed is too simplistic. Are we talking about Baucher's first or second manner? After all, the two methods are almost diametrically opposed. And which period of the Master's career is under scrutiny? The answer to all of these queries determines how one would answer the question of his allegiance (or not) to Mr. Baucher. And I personally think how we answer this loaded question is extremely important and timely for adherents of classical equitation today, now that we are experiencing a huge resurgence of interest in the techniques of François Baucher as well as the work of Nuno Oliveira.

Like most everyone who knew the Master I have my own beliefs on the conundrum, which I will add to the mix further on, but let us begin with Mr. Oliveira's own words on the subject.

"In the 19th century, France had a genius in her midst called François Baucher," the Master writes in *Reflections*. Baucher, explains Oliveira, was molded as a trainer not only by the social and political ideologies of his time, but by the challenge of dealing with an entirely new type of horse to be trained in the high school airs. Heretofore, the Old Masters had used baroque horses, most preferably from the Iberian Peninsula, to express their art. In nineteenth-century

France all that changed, and a new playing field developed with the so-called Anglomania as horses with Thoroughbred blood from England began to become fashionable in France.

"As a result of this 'Anglomania,' " explains Oliveira, "Baucher had to use horses which were different from those types previously chosen, but he was astute enough to add to the enormous works of his predecessors, certain subtleties and intelligent methods which led to working the horse more lightly and intricately. The excesses which are found in his writings are due, above all, to the fact of his birth; of simple stock, he kept a rancor against the nobility who surrounded him in the practice of his art. In order to understand the feelings which animated him it is necessary to have trained many horses of all types, and to know how to understand all the philosophy contained in his works, while putting to one side the excesses produced by the prevailing social order of the times."

Baucher, he continues in *Classical Principles,* had the wisdom to adapt the teachings of the Old Masters of Versailles, using the new types of horses "to create new movements such as flying changes every stride, in order to replace other movements less appropriate for horses which were long and less round. His horsemanship was based on lightness, an indispensable condition for horses like Thoroughbreds and Anglo-Arabs."

Baucher, according to Oliveira, when comparing his first methods with his last teachings, told his disciple L'Hotte that his legs were no longer as tired as they used to be. He called his method of riding after his accident with the infamous chandelier "equitation in bedroom slippers."

It is certainly tempting to draw a few parallels here between François Baucher and Nuno Oliveira. Baucher, the son of a butcher, ironically was born in Versailles when the horsemanship of those revered classical masters of old—indeed, those who had not lost their heads during the purge of the aristocracy in the French Revolution, or fled into exile—had fallen out of favor. He grew up in the eclipse of the old school, and under the rising star of the modern type of military equitation that would become today's Cadre Noir.

He trained horses for the circus, which generally held a more prestigious place in nineteenth-century French equestrian circles than in equestrian venues today.

Nuno Oliveira, as the favored student of Portugal's last Royal Master of the Horse, friend of Portugal's elite equestrian aristocracy but forced to train horses for the circus as a young professional embarking on his equestrian career, must have been in a unique position to understand the evolution of the controversial French trainer. He too burst onto the scene at a pivotal point in equestrian history. After all, "Nuno was starting to be recognized as a riding master just when riding and dressage was changing from an art to a sad mechanical approach," observes his friend and pupil, Professor Jaime Celestino da Costa, in the previously cited French documentary *Nuno Oliveira* (24 images, 2009). Oliveira's horsemanship, while not "better than Miranda's," according to the professor, "was much more comprehensive and up to date."

And so, at a pivotal time in Portugal's equestrian culture, the climate was certainly conducive to an examination of the French innovator Baucher by the rising young Portuguese master, Oliveira.

The teachings of Baucher had stirred heated debate almost since the publication of the first edition of the Frenchman's *New Method of Horsemanship* in 1842. The German trainer Louis Seeger, teacher of Gustav Steinbrecht, whom Nuno Oliveira admired, had even penned a notorious pamphlet which referred to Baucher as "the gravedigger of French equitation." Seeger and Steinbrecht adhered to the old classical exercises such as shoulder-in to achieve balance in motion, denouncing Baucher's flexions of the jaw and neck, which attempted to circumvent resistance and achieve lightness and balance in hand and also from the first moment the horse was mounted.

It is difficult today, with so many training methods and types of horses warring for our attention, to credit the passion, and sometimes vitriol, that surrounded Baucher, but such was the case then, and so it still remains in some equestrian circles.

The late Jean-Claude Racinet, perhaps one of the most recognized authorities on Baucher in America, was also an admirer of Oliveira who researched firsthand the Baucherist influence on the Master.

"Once," he recalls in his previously mentioned article "Was Oliveira a Baucherist?" (*Dressage & CT,* April 1995), "as Michel Henriquet was showing me pictures of his beloved Master, he said in jest, about a photograph in which Oliveira's horse was perhaps somewhat overbent, 'As he was young, my Master had a bout of Baucherism, soon abandoned; youthful indiscretion!' I understood to my dismay that Henriquet was anti-Baucherist and wondered how a same quest, that is, the quest for riding in lightness, had led him to reject Baucher whereas it had led me to acknowledge him!

"A question arises, though. Was this anti-Baucherist stance only the student's or also the Master's? I would have to wait over 12 years before knowing the answer." This came when, following a book review Racinet wrote on *Reflections* for a French magazine, he was invited to Quinta do Brejo to spend several days with the Master. "That morning I had risen very early in order to be in the spectator stand of Oliveira's *manège* by six o'clock," he recalls.

"Oliveira was working at a halt, schooling a horse to the spur. Such a work I had never seen and will probably never see again. It was real clock work: no violence involved, no strength, even obviously no pain for the horse; you could see what the famed expression coined in the 16th century by Antoine de Pluvinel, the 'delicate pinching of the spur,' really meant. Relaxed but willing under his rider, the horse was transformed into a ball of energy.

"When the lesson was over, Oliveira squinted toward me and said, 'This, Mr. Racinet, was some Baucher.' I had noticed.

"The same day in the afternoon, as he was giving lessons, I heard the Master repeat time and again: 'Ask for lightness; ask for lightness. Horsemanship is nothing else but an *'effet d'ensemble'* followed with a release of the aids, one million times!' This, I thought, could hardly be the talk of an anti-Baucherist!"

The style Oliveira exemplified, observes Racinet, "could be considered as a synthesis of the two great French equerries, La Guérinière in the 18th century and Baucher in the 19th."

To illustrate his point, he offers a second example. "The morning after I had seen him work a horse with the spurs the Baucherist way, I saw him engage his mount in a *'terre-à-terre'* (or *'reddop'* for the Germans), a two-beat lateral canter, in a splendid attitude, the torso proudly erect, the leg off the horse and slightly forward, his seat deeply pushed down in the saddle. No aid was visible; the horse was simply jumping laterally like a little rabbit, with energy and lightness. This was Monsieur de Nestier (the Equerry of Louis XV) impersonated. But this was also an illustration of the 'equestrian scale' as described by Baucher, in which the two pans balance each other out so well that the rider's torso becomes the only active aid, whose formidable power carries the horse away in any direction through the most invisible displacement of weight. Had he narrowly stuck to any given school, Oliveira would have belittled his Art."

The debate, according to Racinet, can be summed up as follows. "The 'traditionalists' believe that movement should be a prerequisite to balance; therefore balance is obtained progressively, by implementing movement, a movement abiding by specific patterns, the different figures of *'Manège.'* The Baucherists believe that balance should be a prerequisite to movement; therefore the movement is accepted only to the extent that it does not destroy balance. Balance is lost when lightness is lost. Lightness of the mouth (permanent relaxability of the lower jaw, and this is the core of Baucherism, its creative postulate) is the condition for lightness of the whole.

"This is not a moot debate, since the choice of philosophy will condition the progression in the horse's work. Oliveira, in my opinion, would alternately adhere to either philosophy, depending on the horse he had to work. Basically, he did not think that the two philosophies were exclusive of one another. He, on the contrary, would try to make a blend when it was possible. For instance, when he would choose movement, he sure would have his horses forward, but never in a forceful way."

This duality, observes Racinet, could be a source of dispute among his students, and lasted to the end of his life. "I recently saw two tapes of his from the end of his career," concludes Racinet in his article. "One of them shows him work the 'classical' way, through a pattern of movements 'squeezing' the horse more and more to progressively induce collection (a series of voltes at a canter and counter-canter, travers and renvers at a canter, etc.) until collection is acted out by way of an expressive piaffe.

"On the other tape, he spends the best part of his time at a halt, flexing his horse's neck, *à la* Baucher.

"So it is undeniable that Oliveira's horsemanship had a Baucherist tinge. And it seems to me that in the extent to which he subscribed to the Baucherist philosophy, he was more attracted by the first 'manner' than by the second (although he professed a great admiration for Beudant; but he was leery of raising the neck, one of the main practices of the second 'manner'—I heard him once discard this proceeding)."

In conclusion, "Oliveira admired Baucher," observes Racinet, "and did not dread to put it by script, if necessary, as stands out from the dedication he wrote for me on one of his books: 'To Mr. Racinet, with sincere friendship which I hope will last long, because furthermore a common taste binds us, an admiration for Baucher and his philosophy."

Scholarly Agreement and Debate

As sometimes happens with pivotal issues, Racinet's article spurred much commentary and some lively debate in the equestrian press of the time. Michel Henriquet penned a comment and response, "Maître Oliveira and Baucherism" (*Dressage & CT,* December 1995), in which he points out that his 1965 conversation with Racinet concerned "the photograph of a hyper-Baucherized horse, the lower edge of the neck in the vertical, head rigidly set, elevation of the forehand, but the back hollow and the hocks falling backwards." Oliveira gave him the photo (taken when the Master was only 19) "to serve as an illustration for my work, to point out the negative consequences that could occur were one to follow certain Baucherist methods. Actually, it was Oliveira himself who noted that the photograph represented 'errors of youth.' "

Henriquet tells how he found himself increasingly frustrated after long study under his Baucherist masters. "The equestrian methods of my masters rested exclusively on the precepts of Baucher, who, in attempting to reinvent equitation, had reached a total impasse concerning the principles which the School of Versailles had transmitted via La Guérinière." Without combat or violence, observes Henriquet, "we, nevertheless, always arrived at an easy domination of impulsive horses; but this was often achieved at the expense of impulsion. I was further disturbed by the insufficient suppleness and lack of cadence that resulted. It seemed to me that we were utilizing a whole set of tools but were missing the main piece. The horse's schooling rested solely on the integral application of Baucherization: suppling in place, in hand and mounted; the alternate effects of hand and legs; getting the horse progressively used to the subtle pressure of spurs; the yielding of the hand and legs; and whose main objective was the almost obsessional raising of the horse's neck."

Henriquet writes that he "began to perceive that this raising of the forehand was forced in that it proceeded more from the excessive raising of the hand than the engagement of the haunches obtained by the seat and by Classical suppling. This artificial raising of the hand blocked the horse's back. I also began to be convinced that the Baucherist arsenal did not allow for incurvation or bend as a whole in the forward movement and side stepping." It was during his quest for the "missing link" that he found Oliveira in 1961. "What immediately struck me when I observed the Master work was the wonderful utilization of the essential elements belonging to the School of Versailles: the shoulder-in, executed most vigorously, with aids imperceptible, the development of the forward going motive (propulsive) power, sumptuous cadences, mingling with what is indisputably the legacy of Baucher: the decomposition of contractions by means of gentle halts and departures, the strict application of 'hand without legs, legs without hand,' flexions, in hand and mounted, and coordinated effects (*effets d'ensemble*)."

There in front of him, says Henriquet, he saw the development of the synthesis "of what was best in Traditional French Equitation" with some of Baucher's precepts. "I was so very much aware of witnessing the fusion of these two schools and how well they complemented each other that in my 1965 work *A la Recherche de l'Equitation*, I underscored...the equestrian work of Nuno Oliveira as follows:

"Of Baucherist inspiration, one can consider: Oliveira's absence of opposing hand and legs; the yielding of the horse's haunches, in hand; flexions, in hand, with contracted horses; progressively getting the horse used to the slightest touch of the

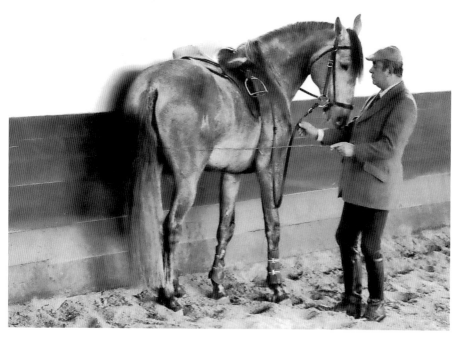

Nuno Oliveira works a young horse in hand, using lateral flexion on the way to achieving suppleness and straightness.

spurs; imparting the *rassembler* to stiff or unbalanced horses; use of *effets d'ensemble* (coordinated effects) which regularize and favor the halt; 'balancing the hand' to straighten the forehand."

In the same work Henriquet also observes, "If the filiation of Oliveira goes back more readily to the tradition and philosophy of La Guérinière than to that of Baucher, it is undeniably that he knew how to preserve those methods of Baucher which were efficacious and compatible with his own conception of equitation."

It is noteworthy here that Henriquet refers to the absolute elevation of the horse's neck, as practiced by many Baucherists of the second manner, and the problems that can occur as a result, especially in horses' backs. Oliveira expressed his own reservations in many of his letters published in Henriquet's book *30 Years with Master Nuno Oliveira* (Xenophon Press, 2011). "When you come back," writes Oliveira to Henriquet, "you will see that I do not work my horses one hundred per cent in accordance with the second manner of Baucher.

"I consider Baucher the greatest equestrian genius, and the principles of his method, the results he obtains and claims, are formidable. However, never moving away from the question of suppleness and lightness, I believe that horses, according to their conformation, their disposition, and their gaits, cannot all be trained by his method, namely, by the maximum elevation of the neck.

"I claim that my horses are raised on the forehand, as you have seen, but there are some [horses that] one must not start out by elevating [the forehand]. They are the ones with necks that are thick, short, and ewe-necked, have a concave back, and weak hocks." In another letter, Oliveira asserts: "It is true that horses, whose necks have been raised prematurely, are not heavy on the hand, but they have an imperfect equilibrium which makes impulsion difficult as they have a locked back. Cadence of the gaits is only possible when the back is supple." In several of his letters to Henriquet, Oliveira also makes clear his dislike for what he refers to as the dreaded "pigeon throat" with incorrect muscling of the neck resulting from excessive elevation.

Even Jean-Claude Racinet, an avowed Baucherist, offers similar cautions regarding the horse's back in "Bauchiveira" (*Dressage & CT*, December 1995), his response to Henriquet's article. The purpose of lifting the head is to elevate the withers, he points out. "It has been known from of old. The Old Masters of the baroque era called it *'soutenir le bout de devant,'* i.e., 'withhold the front end.' Baucher did not invent it. He systematized it, as he did for many other means of the old equitation." Theoretically, continues Racinet, if one lifts the head of a sound horse, "a horse whose spinal column is not the setting of vertebral blockings, the withers are going to rise accordingly. What makes the technique of the lifting of the neck questionable is that many horses have those 'blockings,' and then lifting the neck amounts to hollowing the back and keeping the pelvis flat, quite the opposite of our purpose." No horsemanship, concludes Racinet, can take care of a vertebral problem, which led him into his own research into equine osteopathy. According to Racinet, Dr. Dominique Giniaux (*What the Horses Have Told Me,* 1996, and *Healing Hands,* 1998, Xenophon Press), the French pioneer of equine osteopathy discovered that Baucher's lateral flexions of the neck and jaw may release vertebral blockings from C3 to C7 and T1, "provided one has the 'feel.' And Baucher certainly had it."

So too did Nuno Oliveira. The 2009 French documentary *Nuno Oliveira, Ecuyer of the 20th Century* captures this beautifully with footage of the Master schooling his last horse Bunker demonstrating the value of these flexions: "If shoulder-in was described by Oliveira as the 'aspirin of equitation,' Francois Baucher's flexions proved to be osteopathy for horses. Doctor-Riding Master Oliveira didn't have any fixed method. Each horse is different. Each block, each tension requires a specific remedy. Everything is about how you do it. Bunker's schooling represented the accomplishment of his art for the Portuguese master. 'What a shame my back is giving out,' he said. 'I was just starting to understand riding!' "

Watching Bunker, a Russian horse probably not too far removed from the type of horses Baucher schooled, it is obvious to see the suppleness and lightness achieved through these flexions, and watching him perform all the high school airs in Baucher's horizontal balance is a revelation in what can be achieved with a horse with difficult conformation, balance and movement. The chestnut stallion had gone from an unlevel little horse that no one wanted to a masterpiece under the artist's knowing hand, perhaps the Master's most fitting tribute to the memory of Baucher.

Bridging the Gulf

It is interesting to note that the Master did not see the insurmountable gulf between the old classical school and Baucher that many authors have proclaimed. "Baucher is not so far removed from the spirit of La Guérinière," he tells Henriquet in one of his letters. "If he wanted at all cost to write about a method completely different, what he actually sought to achieve was the lightness of La Guérinière. It is within these two great masters that one must find information that is profitable to art." Only when one works in lightness is one truly involved with equestrian art, concludes Oliveira in his missive. "The rest is the massacre of the innocents."

Also of interest, regarding the classical German author Steinbrecht, I personally once heard the Master refer to him as "Baucher across the Rhine." In *Classical Principles,* he points out that the German master, of the same period as Baucher, "considered one of the great classical masters among present day German horsemen, tried at the end of each chapter of his book to criticize Baucher and his method. But a real connoisseur can see that the two Masters say, in a different way, almost the same thing. They were located on opposite sides of the Rhine: it was a question of nationalism, the result of the times."

My own experiences with the Master and Baucher involved mostly the lateral flexions, both in hand and mounted (which was interesting with the double bridle using only one hand). When I had the chance to question him about the French innovator he told me to use "a little Baucher, only a little." For Raindrop this consisted of the flexions as well as a lot of rein back. Mr. Oliveira spoke of the benefits of rein back for horses which are on the forehand or become heavy on the bit provided it is executed with the horse straight and calm. He mentioned that Baucher spoke about the advantages of reining back for a long time, and that he felt Baucher was right when he finished each lesson with a long, easy rein back.

Of course, he continued, the Old Masters made use of the rein back frequently as well. The Master sometimes had us execute the exercise called *Foule au Reculer*, where we continued the rein back around a circle or serpentine, lightly and with a relaxed jaw. He cautioned us to ask for rein back by the back and legs with very light contact. If done by pulling on the reins, the horse goes backward out of balance and with a hollow back, causing irregular strides. The rein back must not be rushed, he insisted. Done correctly, it would increase the engagement and round the back, allowing the horse to go forward again in perfect balance, and he instructed me to use it frequently during the school exercises with Raindrop.

Regarding the flexions, he mentioned there are many horses who will never be light unless worked with flexions while dismounted, but that they are not necessary for a well-balanced horse with a soft mouth and a good lower neck position. We used the rein back in hand, carefully maintaining the flexion of the jaw and the poll, to prepare Raindrop for the piaffe. If used, the Baucher flexions must be done skillfully and delicately, and he warned us not to fall into the error of softening the neck and allowing it to fall into an incorrect position, which merely justifies critics of the Baucher flexions.

The Master did not agree with the scholars who argue that Baucher did not use shoulder-in, one of the most valuable exercises of the Old School. Exactly what, he asks, was Baucher's leg yield? He repeatedly reminded us that Baucher stressed the value of work in the walk, calling it "the mother of all gaits." In his last work with artist Jean-Louis Sauvat (*Horse and Rider: Annotated Sketches*, Belin, 1990), the Master echoes Baucher when he writes, "In a long life spent working with horses, I have never yet seen any enjoyable work carried out that has not been prepared by the walk."

Relevance Today

In today's equestrian climate, Mr. Oliveira's admonition of "a little Baucher," carefully and appropriately applied, seems particularly wise. He gives only passing mention to Baucher's *ramener outré*. "I have no courage to speak" about the the *ramener outré* he writes in *From An Old Master Trainer to Young Trainers* (Howley & Russell, Australia, 1986), the exaggerated flexion where the horse "put by the action of the 'combined effect,' the lower jaw comes closer to the neck and he savours the bit more actively, and the bits move in the mouth." Although several modern writers see a parallel between this overflexed state in a Baucherized horse of the first manner and the modern extreme of hyperflexion as practiced by some very successful competitive riders during the last decade, I am not so sure.

As Mr. Oliveira points out, Baucher's flexions are mostly used dismounted, in hand, or at the halt and walk when mounted. Some proponents of hyperflexion, on the other hand, often drive the horse fast-forward into a heavy contact, so I personally do not think we can really equate the two extremes, Baucher's overflexed *ramener outré* and modern rollkur, as being the same thing. Needless to say, the Master did not teach either of these extreme techniques.

I find his considered advice to use "a little Baucher" a sensible admonition, a fine middle ground between the extremes of either Baucher's first or second manner, rather like walking the Buddhists' middle path.

In concluding this brief foray into the Baucherist influences on the Master, I personally agree with those writers already quoted who emphasize his skillful blending of the schools of French equitation into a magnificent unity. In *Dressage in the French Tradition* (Xenophon Press, 2011), Diogo de Bragança, a student of Nuno Oliveira, offers a few choice quotes from Baucher when he writes: "The appearance of Baucher's method was connected to his passion for dressage and for the horse. He had come to doubt the methods in use up to that time 'reflecting ignorance and brutality.' He said that 'man has received from the Creator an intelligence superior to that of the animals, not to serve his caprices and to inflict bad treatment on them, but to receive all the services that it is right to ask of them.' "

Such an assessment seems not unlike Nuno Oliveira, who captured the essence of the controversial French master, refining his techniques while discarding the excesses, and in my personal estimation far surpassd the French genius he admired. The legacy of both Versailles and Baucher lived on in Nuno Oliveira, but taken to their next greater evolution, and isn't that precisely the hallmark of a great Master whose teachings truly transcend time?

(Author's Note: Thanks to Susan Racinet and Michel Henriquet for permission to use extensive quotes from the articles mentioned in this chapter, and to the late Ivan Bezugloff, who originally published them in Dressage & CT. *The articles in their entirety may be found reprinted in the archives of* Horses for Life *magazine.)*

Chapter 9

FINDING THE MASTER WITHIN

I have tried in these pages to give an overview of what it was like to study with the "Ecuyer of the 20th Century," as the film by Laurent Desprez describes Nuno Oliveira. In doing so, I have focused mostly on his teachings and influence, a little on his background, and almost nothing at all on the personality and private life of this great equestrian figure of our time.

Often, when a great teacher comes along, there is a tendency to focus more on the messenger than the message, as if insights into a master's particular human virtues or foibles might somehow shed light on the secrets of his mastery. In making the teacher larger than life, as if idolizing a guru, it is all too easy to miss the point and diminish the message.

Instead, I have deliberately chosen to leave Nuno Oliveira himself at a respectful distance, so that his transcendent teachings shine through with little distraction.

An interesting dynamic develops when working with a master trainer, as the student attempts to find his or her own expression within the guidelines of the master's syllabus. "It takes a long time for a rider to mature," Mr. Oliveira observed during one of his last clinics in the United States, and most of us who studied with him have certainly found that to be true.

As the fledgling young trainers mature, some are booted out of the nest whether they feel ready to fly on their own or not. Others leave perhaps prematurely in search of their own inspiration or, sometimes, fame and glory.

Still others bid farewell to their master teacher through extenuating circumstances, such as the teacher's untimely death.

Like many other students, I found myself in the latter category.

Looking back, it is easy to see how Mr. Oliveira began preparing us to be on our own. From the early days of working so frequently under his direction, and having our "homework" checked each time he returned, we moved to less frequent clinics, where we were often left to solve our own difficulties for an extended period.

About the time I began taking various rehab horses to the clinics, I was invited by the Master to what I have always thought of as "the Talk." During one of the evening discussions over wine, Mr. Oliveira took several young trainers aside and asked us a series of questions.

What were our goals? Did we wish to teach? To train horses, either personally or professionally? To compete?

The answers we gave him determined the direction of the conversation. When it came my turn, I answered: "I want to train horses."

He considered the answer with the sincerity it was given, then replied: "Then ride a lot of bad horses. I don't mean ride dangerous horses—you are too valuable now to get hurt—but ride the difficult horses and learn."

He elaborated a little on this theme during our last interview. "Nowadays riders learn one system because if they have a horse that isn't suitable for dressage they sell the horse and get another," he observed. "So instructors now don't know the old systems—for instance, Baucher's flexions—and don't know how to use those systems to improve the horse. Now everybody learns one way, but that doesn't mean that every horse will respond best to that way.

"You can take pieces of a different system and apply them, and riders can understand why they do something from a different system to correct specific problems. But no one teaches the other systems anymore, so riders don't learn to be able to do that."

He encouraged us to keep reading authors from Baucher to Steinbrecht, to keep riding horses of all types, and always to keep an open mind.

"Riders must copy only *good* top riders," he maintained.

In the last years of his life, Mr. Oliveira certified a few of his long-term students to teach under the auspices of his name and his school. Although several are now deceased, including his son Joao, a few still teach around the world.

In addition to those teachers publicly certified to teach from his school, he also quietly sent pupils and their horses to a number of his other longtime students. Much to my surprise, during the last

Joao Oliveira, mounted on a young Portuguese stallion, assists his father in the first lessons breaking in the young horses.

Sue Cromarty, who later married Nuno Oliveira's son, Miguel Oliveira, leads the ride at Quinta do Brejo.

two clinics I attended with him, I found myself in this latter group. I suspect he thought a dressage trainer with one hand probably would not be overflowing with equine clients, but might do better teaching. And so, during my last outings with him I was asked to teach several of the group lessons under his direction. I must admit that while I had never been nervous riding for the Master, not even when I was allowed to ride several of his personal horses, I did feel apprehensive teaching under his eagle eye. Though he said little to me after this challenging experience, I was asked to repeat it several times, so I must have somehow passed muster in his eyes. When he returned to Portugal I was left with a small cadre of students, and I have been teaching ever since.

Evolution

There are some truly valuable techniques I learned under Mr. Oliveira I have found it difficult to share with students. Some are nuances of feeling and a pursuit of lightness that does not interest the average rider, especially those focused on competition.

Other methods, such as longeing with carefully adjusted side reins to help the horse's development, I explore only with longtime students. As a clinician, I have found it unsafe to do so in this era of widespread "natural horsemanship" methods where many horses have been taught to reverse at speed on the longe, and also to go quickly backwards, so I find it prudent in these cases to forgo the use of side reins and concentrate instead on the classical work in hand.

I am sure many of us have encountered similar experiences, and so have learned to adapt what we learned from the Master in the most helpful way in this modern era. Certainly those most interested in competition tend to omit the so-called "equitation of fantasy" such as the Spanish walk and trot, and also the work above the ground, while trainers interested in rehabilitation cases usually focus more on the therapeutic longeing, flexions in hand, and basic lateral work under saddle rather than the high school airs.

I think it is vitally important that those of us who rode with Mr. Oliveira for many years and now teach make it clear we do so from our own experience, and not under his name, except for those very few licensed by his school, especially given the undeniable fact that many people who never actually met the Master have tried to take advantage of his name and reputation.

If it is true that the real impact of a master teacher and his movement is never fully realized until the third generation, then the legacy of Master Nuno Oliveira ultimately rests not just with the memory of his riding and his written works, exceptional as they are, but with the living examples and interpretations of his students and their own pupils, now and to come. Certainly he left many devoted trainers and instructors who honor his name and continue to spread his message of kindness and lightness in dressage around the world. Though his son Joao and daughter-in-law Sue both left us too soon, his grandchildren now carry the torch and the Oliveira name into the next generation.

As the years pass, it has become fashionable for authors far and wide to quote the Master, and so many snippets of his wisdom have made it into the mainstream equestrian press, where photos of him on some of his most famous mounts are often upheld as the classical ideal. Fortunately, just as we went to press, we received news that a new English translation of his *Classical Principles of the Art of Training Horses* is under way, and we can only hope others will follow now that there has been a resurgence of interest in his philosophy and his work.

In contemplating his legacy, now and to come, I am left with a surreal image I experienced shortly after receiving the news of his death. As is widely known, the subconscious mind often processes our deepest feelings and concerns in dream images and events, and I found myself in such a reverie one night. In the dream, I am standing in the arena at the Spanish Riding School in Vienna, which I have visited in real life. A man enters the arena on a white horse, but to my amazement it is not a rider from this hallowed hall on one of the Lipizzaner stallions, but the Master on a classic Lusitano. He rides over to me in the sort of slow motion that happens in dreams and, saying nary a word, dismounts and hands me the reins. Then, still without a good-bye, he turns and walks quietly out of the arena.

The message is clear. After all the beautiful teachings, all the lessons and cherished memories and experiences, one door has closed and a new door is opening.

It is time for the student to find the master within.

Schooling Piaffer

When asked about schooling piaffe with a horse with an unquiet tail, Nuno Oliveira commented that the tail will often become quiet and relaxed as the horse becomes progressively stronger and more comfortable with the work. The photos on this and the following page of the young stallion Tenor, taken by his student Kathy Nelson as the schooling progressed, show the wisdom of this observation.

Piaffer, Tenor, developing strength and relaxation under the Master

Nuno Oliveira with Beau Geste, levade in long reins

Chapter 10

THE MASTER'S LEGACY

(Author's Note: Several of the Master's earliest American students were kind enough to share the tributes in this chapter in memory of the Master. They provide an invaluable historical perspective on the legend, Nuno Oliveira.)

Diana Christensen was one of Nuno's first American students at his teaching facilities at Quinta do Brejo near Malveira, Portugal. She first traveled there to ride with the *Mestre* on his well-trained Lusitano horses in 1976 when his charges were extremely reasonable, at only $5.00 a lesson, or $10.00 per day. And the cost to stay with a family in the village below the farm was only about $1.00 per day for food, room and even laundry.

In 1976, Diana's classes with Nuno were shared with only one other student, so it was almost like one-on-one intensive instruction on his outstanding horses. The horses, Diana said, were an integral part of the schooling and taught the students as much as Nuno.

She returned twice more to Portugal in 1978 and 1985, and in 1982 and 1983 attended two of his clinics in San Antonio, Texas. On the latter date, she trailered two of her own Andalusian horses from Louisiana.

Diana greatly benefited from Nuno's equine philosophy and his methods of teaching and training, all of which provided the basis for the advanced levels of dressage that propelled her to a successful teaching, breeding, and riding career. For 38 years she taught mainly classical dressage at her farm north of New Orleans. In later years, her equine enthusiasm never faded and she was teaching Olympic hopefuls in Texas two weeks before she passed in 2011.

-Arthur Christensen

Nuno Oliveira at St. Agata

by Gretchen Verbonic

The photo of Brother *(next page)* was taken at the small indoor arena that Phyllis Field built, by special arrangement, at the Potomac Horse Center in Maryland. Nuno taught there at least four times a year for at least six years. He also, during that time, trained some typically American horses, *not* horses chosen for their dressage ability, but to prove that he could train them to feel like his Portuguese/Andalusian/Portuguese Arabians/French Thoroughbreds that he had in his school.

Mainly they were trained as school horses, i.e., they knew the movements and performed them willingly if the rider gave some semblance of the correct aids, but with that uniquely Oliveira feeling of a tremendous engine coming up behind the rider. The arena there was named St. Agata after Verdi's (the composer) summer home. The 1974 picture was the first time he came to Potomac and he taught the whole week in a jacket and tie! The picture is of my registered Thoroughbred show hunter turned into a Prix St. Georges level dressage horse. I later worked a Swedish Warmblood and a Dutch Warmblood with Nuno showing both at Grand Prix and being long-listed by the USET with both.

The pictures in Quinta do Brejo are obviously the arena and stables at Nuno's farm, Quinta do Brejo, just outside of the very small village of Avessada in Portugal. I vividly remember walking from my rented house in Avessada in early morning up the dusty road to the school and being joined by herdsmen and their sheep. Nuno's classical music, that he had playing when he schooled horses, could be heard clearly. As I smiled profusely and tried to communicate in my pidgin Portuguese, I'm sure I saw in those simple men's faces the following thought: "All of you are nuts!"

I had to include one picture of the charming donkeys that populated all the roads. They wore little chicken wire muzzles so they wouldn't eat their loads of cut grass.

I trained in Portugal twice with Nuno, in 1976 with the help of an Asmis Scholarship and in 1977 with a Field Scholarship. I also sold an American Thoroughbred horse that I trained to Ms. Field's daughter who competed him in France.

Le Maître, as we learned to call Nuno, was always a perfect gentleman, polite, kind, interesting, fun and giving. Whenever I am with a horse, *Le Maître* is with me, as are so many of the things he taught us all. I have those ideas "in my pocket" where he said to keep them for use as we needed them. But I never was able to "install" the same powerful engine in my horses that Nuno could.

Nuno Oliveira instructs Gretchen Verbonic on her Thoroughbred, Brother, at the St. Agata arena in Maryland during the early 1970s at one of his first American clinics.

Phyllis Field, who sponsored Nuno Oliveira's clinics in Maryland for many years, rides a ballotade on Levante, as captured by Katherine Nelson in Portugal at Quinta do Brejo.

Nuno Oliveira's Legacy

by Katherine Nelson

Nuno Oliveira was a phenomenon the likes of which I am not likely to see again. In the 36 years since my return from Portugal, riding twice a day on his beautifully trained school horses for nearly two years, I have had many horses, many important coaches, and much instruction. I can only say that each day that I put my foot into a stirrup I thank my lucky stars and Nuno Oliveira. I was a daily witness to his training genius. I saw him do so many "impossible" things—like passage to piaffe transitions where he put down the curb rein first, then picked up the snaffle rein, so that the actual transition was performed with no reins.

Seldom are brilliant riders also such brilliant teachers. Nuno's teaching style was certainly idiosyncratic. He might appear to be napping, having said not a word for many minutes—then suddenly crack an eyelid and say something like "left hand more to right," and solve all of your horse's problems. In America, he transformed a motley group of us naïve riders and our miscellaneous horses into a coterie of capable trainers and schoolmaster mounts. Through his kind generosity and that of Mrs. Phyllis Field, I was able to continue occasional lessons in the US and Portugal until 1987, and by then the truths about horse training were starting to sink in.

If I had to distill what I have learned exclusively from Nuno, I would have to say it is the intricate interdependency of straightness on suppleness; of impulsion on straightness; and of collection on impulsion. Not the idea of it—the feel of it. I can hear his voice always reminding me in answer to a question, "It depends of (sic) the horse. Every horse is different."

NUNO

by Eloise King

(This moving tribute was written in the 1980s only a few years before the Master's death. -Stephanie Millham)

The man is the most perfect rider in the world today. I dare say that training all movements, even those above ground, is simple. It is easy. He is perfect, and that is the key to his training. His perfection leaves the horse with no doubt, and, in a sense, no choice. When Nuno puts his body in "shoulder-in," the horse must also put his body in "shoulder-in." When Nuno sits in "two track," the horse gives that first step in "two track" and he is rewarded. So, next time, it's two or three or four steps, but never more than the horse can comfortably give. Never more steps, never more bend. The footfall is correct and the movement grows. It grows, because it's always rewarded; never punished, but allowed; never forced, always correct.

Correct and Patient

The horse is trying, he is attentive. Nuno is patient. The horse gives—a weight change or relax a step—it doesn't matter, the Master felt it. The horse felt the reward, and there is always "again."

"Again," what is "again"? It is "again."

When all is in total relaxation, totally comfortable in mind and body, then and only then will he ask "again." And again, the reward follows the horse's response, not the movement.

The movement is being trained, not demanded. It might not even happen for a day, or two, or longer. Onlookers do not see the building and preparation he is giving the young stallion. But, on the day he rides that horse and "bingo," it's there, they see *that.* In three months, when the movement is totally confirmed—flowing forward, cadenced, relaxed, collected, in self-carriage—now the world sees it. The world is still asking, "How? Where did it come from?" I answer that by saying, "It came from perfection." The man built it; the man is perfect."

I learned from watching him train and from training my own horses under his quiet eye. Sometimes for weeks he said nothing to me. I tried to use "again," never "more," never "stronger," but for me, "again" took much longer, because for me to ask "again" correctly, I would first have to work at getting myself correct. First correct *me*; first I must be correct before I ask "again," but this time let me stay correct, let me stay relaxed in my aids while I ask "again." The horse can only hear your aids if nothing else is being said. You must not change the rhythm, speed, or carriage as you give an aid. The aid may cause a change and the trainer must accept that change even if it's not what he intended. If the trainer does not accept that change—if he chases or holds back the animal—he will no longer have the horse's attention on the aids he's giving. While the aids are being applied, the trainer must stay relaxed in the aids. I must repeat that you must think of correcting yourself first; not in punishing the horse for giving the wrong response. Often the problem lies in the aids being too strong, so again think of relaxing; go back to the perfect walk or trot—not just a step or two—but back to rhythm and cadence. Circle, and this time give your aids more gently and let the horse have time to respond. Stop being in a hurry. You say, "Again takes too long." I have watched trainers come and teach a student and the same horse once a week, for one, two, three and four years, still trying to get the perfect trot on a circle with "on the bit" being the lesson. Forty-five minutes later, the trainer is saying "good, good, good," and if he were scoring that "Good" on a training or first level test, he'd be writing a six. Ah, but those are the experts, not the artists or trainers, in my eyes.

In watching Nuno, I just kept seeing things grow. Movements, impulsion, muscles, cadence, rhythm; all these things brought about self-carriage as the upper level frame developed (which people associate with dressage). I saw his horses were always in self-carriage from the moment he mounted. He worked his horses in hand and carefully set his horse up at the side of the ring to accept his weight. Again, his seat is perfect. The horse accepts the weight with the muscles for carrying his rider, already soft and supple. Nuno's weight is also soft and supple. When he sits tall and correct in the saddle, as he does for piaffe and passage, his pelvis has stayed just as soft as it is for an extension, but he has straightened his back and literally lifted and filled his chest and diaphragm with air as only the best opera singers can do. He is ready, "one with his horse," as he moves off in a walk and thus he stays "one with his horse" until he has gotten off.

But all this has started because I was thinking of a day he had lunged a young horse. The horse, even for Nuno, was powerful, headstrong, wanting to be heavy, wanting to be a bad-moving stallion. In the course of a month he had truly, and with no doubt in his mind, the horse's mind, or any spectators' minds, put "forward" on the stallion. The horse understood "forward." When the horse had started out saying, "O.K., I'll go," he merely went faster and faster—not "forward." That horse got sent "forward," and he went faster. The side reins were flopping, the sweat was pouring out of him, and he still went faster. Then *bang*, like a shot from a gun, the horse had figured it out. It was all there. He came to the side rein, his back came up. His breathing changed. Now he had rhythm, he was "forward." Yes, it took forty minutes, maybe longer. He was rewarded. Then Nuno changed directions and off the horse went, as though nothing had been learned. Nuno was behind him again, just asking "forward" and letting the poor guy figure it out. The horse figured it out, sooner this time, and got his reward. Reverse. Again, a period of confusion, but very soon, "forward." Reward and reverse. Soon the horse started each new direction "forward." The horse's "forward" got slower—not lazy, but more relaxed, with lovely even strides and breathing. And so it continued until the horse was completely cooled out, breathing normally and quietly. The cooling out was entirely performed on the lunge line at the trot. Nuno did not walk him to quiet him; he was cooled and relaxed by "forward," rhythm, and honesty. The horse had no doubt. He had been pushed, but never confused, never punished, never treated dishonestly in that lesson. It was a lesson in "forward." This particular horse had to have this lesson two more times, and that is very rare.

It is a lesson I've often seen Nuno give. And it's necessary for many a mare as it is a stallion. With this particular stallion, it made him a safe and honest horse. Otherwise, he would have become dangerous and untrainable. Over the years, I've seen potential or brilliant horses never realized because the first lesson in "forward" never happened. For those horses discipline and force was part of every dealing. In the stall, tacking up, lungeing, loading, riding, showing, jumping. Discipline and force had become routine. It becomes the horse leading the lesson and the trainer is trained by the horse.

With Nuno that stallion is now a decent mover. He does not curl and climb with his front legs. They are moving from the shoulder and they come free and forward to the ground. They land with a lightness I would never have thought possible one day ago.

Then there was the day Nuno spent an hour and forty-five minutes coming out on a diagonal and letting that same horse lengthen. He also let it fall around the corner, then get its balance and cadence and lengthen on the next diagonal. Soon the gallery were all "oohing" and "aahing," because the horse was giving lovely extensions. He was still falling around the corner. The audience was so happy with the extensions and they "oohed" and "aahed" louder, so he would hear, reward his horse and stop. I was totally aware that the extensions he developed were only a wonderful by-product of what he was trying to teach. I realized I was the only one riding with him in my head, feeling his gentle aid to come back. The first time the horse quit running around the corner and listened to his aid, instantly the reins dropped and the master said "ahhh" in his low rewarding sound. Our eyes met and, alas, only one other person was still sitting there. The rest had never seen the magic moment. Nuno walked over and rang the bell. He returned a hot, tired, but happy horse to the groom.

The next day, work as usual—walk work was followed by trot, and when he lengthened the diagonal and the horse came back on an effortless light aid, reins dropped and the horse went home. Yes, Nuno is a genius, but first he's honest and so the answer is "*yes.*" I'd like to be his horse. I would not be doing the same circle with the same rider, in the same ring, on the same day of the week, at the same hour, and after forty minutes be told "good," year in and year out—and for competition's sake be put "on the bit" with impulsion. "*No*," I would not like to be that trainer's horse.

"*Yes*," I'd rather be an artist's horse and soon be dancing through life, my muscles getting stronger each day and I becoming a stronger and more supple athlete. No vet would be x-raying my hock. My conformation would in no way limit my ability to be correct. I'd become a joy and I'd become a work of art with my master above me.

Why did I go to Portugal?

To watch a genius work. *And watch I did.* I could care less about changes at every stride, and soon was bored watching passage in class. Never did my eyes move off Nuno during the four weeks I was there. No, I never asked a question; I watched. I saw horses ask questions. I saw Nuno answer them.

Eloise King on her Arab, Gindari, in levade

A Master in the Truest Sense of the Word

by Linda Konigsberg

In my more than sixty years, there has been no other person who has been more instrumental in my life as a rider, trainer, and instructor than Nuno Oliveira. I first met Nuno when I took a month's vacation to Europe to see the 1972 Olympic Games, followed by two weeks in Portugal working on dressage in Nuno's Lisbon riding school. I had seen horses perform in the Olympic dressage venue, but that was no comparison to what I saw in Nuno's school—levade, ballotade, extended passage, forty one-tempi's in a small circle and cantering backwards, to name a few. I came to understand that Nuno found the limitations of competition confining, and I knew then that I wanted to learn as much as possible from this true master.

Nuno had a unique way of teaching in that quite often, rather than making corrections, he would wait until something was finally right before making any affirmation. This helped to teach riders a better sense of feel and timing. But more than learning in riding lessons, I think my education was most enhanced by watching him train his horses and those of his students. On most occasions, his techniques were successful; but on those rare occasions when something didn't meet his satisfaction, he always had multiple methods to reach the same result. It was amazing to see the camaraderie he had with his horses—stallions free in the arena always looked to wherever Nuno was in the school, as if there was some inaudible conversation going on between them.

Nuno Oliveira was a Master in the truest sense of the word. His love for his horses and his art was undeniable and blatantly obvious. I was one of the most fortunate people in the world to have known him and to have benefited from his knowledge. The dressage world would be far better today were he still with us.

A Love of Opera

Nuno Oliveira was particularly inspired by Italian opera, most notably the compositions by Guiseppe Verdi. The hills around his school resounded with classical music. Here he sings a work by his favorite composer along with student and friend Charles Osborne.

In *Classical Principles* he quoted a letter written by Verdi in 1874: "Perhaps I will not have the strength to arrive where I wish to arrive: but I know perfectly well what I wish to achieve."

As Mozart Was to Music

by Mary Rose

As a child growing up in Oxford, England, I was aware of Nuno Oliveira and his work in Portugal but only through books and articles about him. When I first went to Portugal in 1956 to stay with the family of a high school classmate I asked about the possibility of visiting his school, but my hosts were non-horsey so it didn't happen.

In 1966 Nuno Oliveira came to London to give an exhibition in front of the queen at the Horse of the Year Show. By this time I was a full-time riding teacher/horse trainer with my BHSI qualification and much more aware of the horse world in general. I realized that Nuno's exhibition (which was done in typical costume and with a flamboyance unappreciated by many staid British horsemen) had earned him a dismissive reputation with some as "circus" and therefore not "classical." However his exhibition coupled with Nuno's generosity in sharing his magnificent stallions with the general public made me a lifelong devotee and determined to train with him.

I moved to the United States in 1967and life intervened so it was not until 1975 that I was able to make my dream of studying with Nuno Oliveira a reality. I spent a month in Portugal in the spring of that year and my life was transformed forever. I had already been awarded a Fellowship by the British Horse Society in 1970 and was considered an advanced rider/trainer. I had also been fortunate to receive quality teaching and mentoring by many renowned experts. But when I first sat astride one of Nuno's wonderful teaching stallions—Dom Achille was my first mount—I realized I knew absolutely nothing!

What did I expect to see as I watched Nuno ride and train all day, every day? Having witnessed fourteen consecutive pirouettes followed by a bow to the queen, not to mention passage, piaffe and Spanish walk and Spanish trot in the performance in 1966 I probably expected to see him working on "airs" all day every day

121

but instead what I saw was endless, patient, perfect work on the basics of correct circles, shoulder-in, half pass and lengthening and shortening of the frame. Our small group took two lessons each day (except Sunday) riding Nuno's amazing horses. His teaching style was unique. He never told you how to do something (as is often attempted by other instructors) that he wanted. The lessons were all conducted in French (in which, fortunately, I was fluent) and all started with the "work in walk."

The walk we were expected to use was the highly collected "school walk" and the "work" consisted of circles, shoulder-in, half pass, etc. This was followed by the "work in trot" performed still as a "ride" (one behind the other at about one horse's length). The arena was the classical size, 15 meters by 30 meters, so much smaller than we were used to at home. Only for the work in canter did we ride individually; the group lined up in the center of one end and each student cantered in turn. After the canter Nuno would again work individually with each student, depending on which horse they were riding, on piaffe, passage or, for myself on one glorious day, levade.

Nuno introduced me to a world of connection with the horses that I had only dreamed of. This is where I started to learn to become completely *one* with the horse, to ride with the mind and almost without legs or hands. Each of us riding for Nuno would strive our hardest to hear him say "Yes!" which signaled we had performed some move correctly.

Fortunately Nuno started coming regularly to Maryland in the late 1970s and 1980s and I was able to attend his clinics and ride my beautiful imported Lusitano stallion with him at Potomac Horse Center.

I remain to this day his most ardent devotee. I conjure him up to stand at the end of my arena as I ride every day. I strive to live up to the ideals he taught and to pass his magic on to my students. I know he changed many lives. Such talent comes rarely—as Mozart was to music, Nuno was to riding, and this world is forever changed.

Observations on a Legacy

by Holly Hansen

When one is in the presence of a true Master, it elicits a feeling so extraordinarily profound that it resonates pure truth. Having met *Mestre* Oliveira only once in the early 80s, I experienced just such a feeling during a clinic in the United States. I could only imagine what it must have been to actually study under him in Portugal until I met one of his longtime pupils and devotees.

The Foundation for Classical Horsemanship dedicated a classical *Pas de Trois* to the legacy of Nuno Oliveira at their annual symposium in 2009 on the 20th anniversary of the Master's death. Volunteer riders from left to right are Holly Hansen, president, Lorna Russell, and Sandy Cooper, all riding Lusitanos.

I had been with horses of various breeds my entire life, but had never been introduced to this level of sensitivity using training techniques that with the greatest tact and finesse, carefully and slowly developed the mental and physical aspect of the horse taking great care to not upset his gentle and sometimes very delicate nature. It was a true revelation and the art of horsemanship took on a whole new meaning.

Since first meeting Stephanie Millham over three decades ago, I have had the great honor of training many youngsters, mostly Andalusians and Lusitanos, as well as rehabilitating far too many horses who had not been started according to the classical

Shoulder-in, classical *Pas de Trois* dedicated to Nuno Oliveira by the Foundation for Classical Horsemanship

principles. Each time Stephanie came to give me a lesson on one of these magnificent horses, I realized how much I had to learn. With kindness and compassion, Stephanie imparted her knowledge as she watched me with these amazing creatures who, although broken, seemed to know intuitively that we were trying to help them. I learned early on in my lessons that the horses knew my intentions, and each schooling session overcame their past barbaric and hasty training and they became mentally more attuned with their rider. I had studied with many other people to learn about technique and timing, but never before had been exposed to the level of feel and sensitivity. I began to understand through Stephanie's watchful eye and careful instruction that intelligence is paramount and controlling one's own emotion was critical.

I understood that if I were to truly be able to help these beautiful horses, I had to stay in the moment and not be outraged about the brutality that they had previously been made to endure. "Where violence begins, art ends." How many times over the years of watching what goes on at shows and clinics has this been apparent. If only these riders could have been exposed early on to someone who truly understood the nature of the horse and had the skill and experience to make them aware of enlightened equitation, biomechanics and classical techniques that could make the horse stronger through gentle gymnasticizing without upsetting their mind.

The equestrian world we live in today has many great advantages with the development of veterinary science, nutrition, farrier care and our ability to, with the click of a button, get inundated with information about just about anything. But information is not knowledge and I believe that all one needs to do is study history to see the possible danger of fads and modern trends if one is focused on winning a competition rather than what is truly good for the horse. Horses have not changed over the years, but our use of them has. Reading the classic books on horsemanship, watching DVD's and being in the presence of a teacher who is truly dedicated to the preservation of the *art of classical horsemanship* is as important now as ever before. Stephanie Millham and others like her are keeping that art alive. It is a long road and one must have a profound love of horses and strive to enjoy the journey. And realize that one lifetime is not enough.

Thank you, Stephanie, from the bottom of my heart for all the horses that you have helped and the riders you have enlightened. Your enthusiasm, intelligence, quietness and sense of culture have not gone unnoticed.

Columbus, NC, December 2012

Stephanie Millham, master of ceremonies for the Foundation, shown in passage on the Andalusian stallion Afamado, exhibition in 18th century costume.

AFTERWORD

The heartfelt tributes from a small sampling of Nuno Oliveira's students in the previous chapter attest to his lasting influence in American dressage. When one considers the group is made up of Grand Prix trainers and competitors who have also held, variously, USEF judging credentials at the highest levels, USDF and also BHS instructor certifications, such glowing praise may seem even more noteworthy. But this is in no way unusual once it is understood that most of the Master's long-term American students reached the highest levels of dressage, some even going on to represent their country as riders or coaches, though not all have acknowledged the Master so publicly.

Almost twenty years after Mr. Oliveira's death, a small group of his students and admirers began to hold an annual educational classical symposium to honor the traditions of his teachings, and thus was born the nonprofit, tax-exempt Foundation for Classical Horsemanship. The Foundation dedicated its second symposium in 2009, which coincided with the 20th anniversary of Nuno Oliveira's death, to the memory of the Master who so inspired its founders and its volunteer clinicians and lecturers.

One of the Foundation's founding board members and the current president, Holly Hansen, penned the preceding notes about training in the Oliveira tradition as a second generation student, without the benefit of the Master but studying his writings and working with several of his students. We have chosen to close with her observations about the importance of his legacy.

Thanks to dedicated riders such as Holly and the Foundation's other volunteer riders and trainers, students of Mr. Oliveira all over the world, his family and his friends, his legacy continues unabated into the twenty-first century at a time when it is perhaps needed more than ever before.

Stephanie Millham

Memories of *Quinta do Brejo*

The Master's outdoor arena, at the top of the hill

A student (Alice Loomis) passages past the Master
seated above in the gallery.

Nuno Oliveira instructs a student in levade on Jabute.

On the Road to Avessada

Reflections

"Why do you ride?

You ride because you love your horse."

"There is only one equitation—good or bad."

Nuno Oliveira

"Nuno Oliveira showed me the visual and practical execution of a dream. The performance I saw in front of my eyes went beyond my wildest dreams. I've never seen anything that got as close to an ideal that indeed I always thought was utopian."

Michel Henriquet

Quoted in *Nuno Oliveira* (24 images)

"It really was an insight into academic equitation. That's probably what I like most. But in terms of balance and collection it was an illustration that we hadn't seen for a very long time, if we'd ever seen it at all. Everyone always wanted to ride in lightness and balance. But when someone succeeds in doing what he says then it's very comforting. It proves that it's possible."

General Pierre Durand

Nuno Oliveira (24 images)

In Loving Tribute

Nuno Oliveira

1925-1989

"...and at the end of the ride,
give the reins,
caress,
say 'thank you' to your horse...."

Nuno Oliveira, Reflections of a Master

The Master's Works

Books by or in collaboration with Nuno Oliveira which have been translated into English are listed below. Most are currently out of print and unavailable except where noted, although most French and German editions are still readily available.

Haute École: Forty-three Photographs of Horses Taught and Mounted by Nuno Oliveira, ©Nuno Oliveira (J.A. Allen & Co. Ltd., London, 1965). Out of print.

Reflections on Equestrian Art, Nuno Oliveira (J.A. Allen & Co. Ltd., London, 1976). Reprinted in 2001 and 2010. Currently available from the publisher and most online booksellers.

Notes and Reminiscences of a Portuguese Rider, Nuno Oliveira (Private Edition, 1982). Out of print.

Classical Principles of the Art of Training Horses, Nuno Oliveira (Howley and Russell, Victoria, AU, 1983). English edition, currently out of print.

Classical Principles of the Art of Training Horses, Volume II: From an Old Master Trainer to Young Trainers, Nuno Oliveira (Howley & Russell, Caramut, AU, 1986). Out of print.

Horses and Their Riders, Nuno Oliveira (Howley and Russell, Caramut, AU, 1988). Out of print.

Horse and Rider: Annotated Sketches, Nuno Oliveira and Jean-Louis Sauvat (Editions Belin, Paris, 1990). English and French. Copies available from a few French booksellers.

The Truth in the Teaching of Nuno Oliveira, Nuno Oliveira and Eleanor Russell (Eleanor Russell, Tenterfield, AU, 2001). Available from Xenophon Press.

BIBLIOGRAPHY

In addition to the Master's works, the following references were also consulted. Volumes listed are the editions used.

Beudant, Étienne, *Horse Training, Out-door and High School,* Charles Scribner's Sons, New York, 1931

Bragança, Diogo de, *Dressage in the French Tradition*, Xenophon Press, Franktown, VA, 2011

Coux, Antoine de, *The Wisdom of Master Nuno Oliveira,* Xenophon Press, Franktown, VA 2012

Desprez, Laurent, *Nuno Oliveira, The Riding Master of the 20th Century*, DVD, 24 images, 2009

Nuno Oliveira, 20 Years After, DVD, 24 images, 2009

Graciosa, Filipe, *Escola Portuguesa de Arte Equestre,* Medialivros, S.A., Lisbon, 2004

Guérinière, François Robichon de la, *École de Cavalerie*, *Part II* Xenophon Press, Franktown, VA 1992

Henriquet, Michel, *Henriquet on Dressage,* Trafalgar Square Publishing, North Pomfret, VT, 2004

  30 Years with Master Nuno Oliveira, Xenophon Press, Franktown, VA, 2011

Heuschmann, Gerd, *Balancing Act, The Horse in Sport–An Irreconcilable Conflict?* Trafalgar Square, North Pomfret, VT, 2012

Loch, Sylvia, *Dressage*, Trafalgar Square Publishing, North Pomfret, VT, 1990

  The Classical Rider, Trafalgar Square Publishing, North Pomfret, VT, 1997

The Royal Horse of Europe, J. A. Allen, London, 1986

Karl, Philippe, *Long Reining*, A & C Black, London, 1992

Nelson, Hilda, *François Baucher, The Man and His Method,*
    Xenophon Press Franktown, VA, 2013

    Alexis-François L'Hotte, The Quest for Lightness in Equitation,
    J. A. Allen, London, 1997

Pluvinel, Antoine de, *The Maneige Royal*, Xenophon Press,
    Franktown, VA, 2010

Racinet, Jean-Claude, *Another Horsemanship,* Xenophon Press, 1994

    Racinet Explains Baucher, Xenophon Press, 1997

Steinbrecht, Gustav, *The Gymnasium of the Horse,* Xenophon Press,
    Franktown, VA, 2011

Van Schaik, Dr. H.L.M., *Misconceptions and Simple Truths in
    Dressage,* J. A. Allen, London, 1986

PHOTO CREDITS

Cover

Nuno Oliveira, Piaffe in Hand, photo by Kathy Cleaver

Chapter 1

Portrait, page 2, photo by Stephanie Grant Millham

Gallery, page 3, photo by Stephanie Grant Millham

Quinta do Brejo, page 6, photo by Stephanie Grant Millham

Early morning, page 7, photo by Stephanie Grant Millham

Three stallions, page 8, photo by Stephanie Grant Millham

Half-pass, page 10, photo by Stephanie Grant Millham

School trot, page 12, photo by Kathy Cleaver

Chapter 2

Piaffe, page 16, photo by Stephanie Grant Millham

Ulysses, page 18, photo by Pedro Villalva, courtesy of Pureza Oliveira

Tesouro, page 23, photo by Pedro Villalva, courtesy Pureza Oliveira

Dr. Guilherme Borba, page 25, photo by Sally Cleaver

Tesouro piaffe, page 27, photo by Pedro Villalva, courtesy Pureza Oliveira

Chapter 3

Alter Real stallion, page 28, photo by Sally Cleaver

Quadrille, page 29, photo by Sally Cleaver

Piaffe between the pillars, page 32, photo by Sally Cleaver

Dr. Filipe Graciosa, page 33, photo by Sally Cleaver 1998

Chapter 8

Chapter 9

Chapter 10

Resting donkey, page 130, photo by Stephanie Grant Millham

Avessada donkey, page 130, photo by Gretchen Verbonic

Tribute, page 133, photo by Stephanie Grant Millham

Reverie, page 134, photo by Stephanie Grant Millham

Back Cover

Stephanie Millham, photo by Ernie Millham